D0065989

The Anna Karenina Fix

The Anna Karenina Fix

Life Lessons from Russian Literature

VIV GROSKOP

Abrams Press, New York

Copyright © 2018 Viv Groskop

Cover design: gray318

Published in 2018 by Abrams Press, an imprint of ABRAMS. All rights reserved. No portion of this book may be reproduced, stored in a retrieval system, or transmitted in any form or by any means, mechanical, electronic, photocopying, recording, or otherwise, without written permission from the publisher.

First published in the United Kingdom by Penguin Books Ltd.

The publisher is grateful for permission to quote from: *A Calendar of Wisdom* by Leo Tolstoy, translated by Roger Cockrell (Alma Classics, 2015). Reprinted by permission of Alma Books Ltd; *Anna Karenina* by Leo Tolstoy, translated by Richard Pevear and Larissa Volokhonsky (Penguin Classics, 2000). Translation and editorial copyright © Richard Pevear and Larissa Volokhonsky, 2000, reprinted by permission of Penguin Random House; *Doctor Zhivago* by Boris Pasternak, translated by Max Hayward and Manya Harari (Vintage Classics, 2002). English translation copyright © Harvill, 1957, reprinted by permission of Penguin Random House; "Requiem" and "The Guest" from *The Complete Poems of Anna Akhmatova*, edited by Roberta Reeder and translated by Judith Hemschemeyer (Canongate, 2000). Reprinted by permission of Canongate Books; *Eugene Onegin* by Alexander Pushkin, translated by Charles Johnston (Penguin Classics, 2003). Copyright © Charles Johnston, 1977, 1979, reprinted by permission of Penguin Random House; *Crime and Punishment* by Fyodor Dostoevsky, translated by Richard Pevear and Larissa Volokhonsky (Vintage Classics, 1993). Reprinted by permission of Penguin Random House; *Three Sisters* by Anton Chekhov, translated by Julius West (Digireads, 2008). Reprinted by permission of Digireads.com; *One Day in the Life of Ivan Denisovich* by Alexander Solzhenitsyn, translated by Ralph Parker (Penguin Modern Classics, 2000). Copyright © Victor Gollancz Ltd, 1962, reprinted by permission of Penguin Random House; *The Master and Margarita* by Mikhail Bulgakov, translated by Michael Glenny (The Harvill Press, 1988). Copyright in the English translation © The Harvill Press and Harper and Row Publishers, 1967, reprinted by permission of Penguin Random House; *Manuscripts Don't Burn: Mikhail Bulgakov: A Life in Letters and Diaries* by J. A. E. Curtis (Bloomsbury, 2012). Reprinted by kind permission of Julie Curtis; *Dead Souls* by Nikolai Gogol, translated by Robert A. Maguire (Penguin Classics, 2004). Copyright © Robert A. Maguire, 2004, reprinted by permission of Penguin Random House; *War and Peace* by Leo Tolstoy, translated by Anthony Briggs (Penguin Classics, 2007). Translation and editorial material copyright © Anthony Briggs, 2005, reprinted by permission of Penguin Random House.

Every effort has been made to trace copyright holders and to obtain their permission for the use of copyrighted material. The publisher apologizes for any errors or omissions and would be grateful to be notified of any corrections that should be incorporated in future editions of this book.

Library of Congress Control Number: 2017956770

ISBN: 978-1-4197-3272-0
eISBN: 978-1-68335-344-7

Printed and bound in the United States

10 9 8 7 6 5 4 3 2 1

Abrams books are available at special discounts when purchased in quantity for premiums and promotions as well as fundraising or educational use. Special editions can also be created to specification. For details, contact specialsales@abramsbooks.com or the address below.

ABRAMS The Art of Books
195 Broadway, New York, NY 10007
abramsbooks.com

Contents

v

Introduction

'"Classic"—a book which people praise but don't read.'

Mark Twain

An enemy of baked goods of all kinds, Tolstoy was not one of those insufferable people who breeze through life unencumbered by frustration and angst. Comfortingly enough, he was a person who struggled to understand why, at times, life felt intensely painful, even when nothing that bad was happening. His empathy for the pain of the human condition is surprising in some ways, because he lived a monastic existence and indulged in few, if any, pleasures. Unlike the rest of us, he really had very little to feel bad about. Tolstoy was very much not a doughnuts-and-beer kind of guy. He only ate cake if it was a family birthday, and then it had to be a particular cake, his wife's Anke pie, a sour lemon tart named after a family doctor. Mostly, he ate simply and repetitively. One of the researchers at the Tolstoy Museum at his estate in Yasnaya Polyana recently uncovered evidence of his fifteen favourite egg dishes, which he ate in rotation. These included scrambled eggs with dill, and peas with eggs. He didn't drink alcohol. He didn't eat meat. And yet still he frequently felt that he was a terrible person.

Perhaps as a result of this tortured way of thinking, long before self-help manuals became hugely popular in the early twentieth century, Tolstoy had already written one of his own. It was full of the sort of inspirational quotes we're now used to

I

seeing on fridge magnets and as advertisements for mindfulness retreats. Some of the sayings are his own quotes:

We only truly come alive in ourselves when we live for others.

If a rich man is to be truly charitable, he will give away all his wealth as soon as possible.

In itself, work is not a virtue, but it is an essential condition of a virtuous life.

The other sayings are from writers and thinkers who inspired him: Rousseau, Plutarch, Pascal, Epictetus, Marcus Aurelius, Emerson, John Ruskin and Henry David Thoreau among others, as well as quotations from the Talmud and the Bible. In Tolstoy's defence, *A Calendar of Wisdom* was deeply serious and well meant. The book itself is calming, fascinating and often unintentionally entertaining: 'If you are in the grip of carnal passions and overwhelmed by them, you will become entwined in the creeping bindweed of suffering' – Buddhist wisdom. (Bring on the carnal passions, I say. Worry about the bindweed later.) Also known as *A Circle of Readings* or *The Thoughts of Wise People*, *A Calendar of Wisdom* consisted of a page of inspiring quotes for each day of the year, collected by Tolstoy over sixteen years and a popular edition was published in 1912, two years after his death.

A lot of the quotes directly contradict the messages of today's self-help movement, which encourages us to devote ourselves passionately to the art of learning to love ourselves, or, at the very least, to move away from self-hate. In *A Calendar of Wisdom*, it's the other way round. Pride and a love of the self are wrong; and if we are going to hate anyone, we should hate ourselves. (It literally says this. This sentiment is very typical of Tolstoy, who disliked doing anything pleasant, easy or fun.) Tolstoy prescribes an extreme, ascetic way of life, where lustful desires are especially dangerous and overeating is a sin because it denotes a lack of self-respect. Here are some of his other entries. On 4 June: 'Because Christianity has become perverted, we now lead a life that has become worse than a pagan's.' Some of his edicts are painfully enigmatic. On 27 October: 'The light remains the light, even though a blind man cannot see it.' And anything relating to women is generally bad news. On 2 June: 'A woman has a great responsibility: to give birth. But she doesn't give birth to ideas – that is the responsibility of men.'

Tolstoy saw these quotes as a guide to life at a time of crisis: a gathering of 'a circle of the best writers' whose ideas would lead to salvation. As Roger Cockrell, translator of the latest edition of the *Calendar* in English, writes, Tolstoy's overall aim is 'to urge us all to strive, through unrelenting effort, for self-improvement'. I am not saying that Tolstoy is Oprah Winfrey with a beard. (Well, I am saying that a bit. And in any case, it's just fun to think of the two of them together.) But he had an instinct for the sort of thinking that would become hugely popular a century later. And he had a strong conviction that the only way to fight back against the pressures of modern life was to define the right life lessons and apply them to yourself. This book follows the same impetus and aims to channel the Oprah side of Tolstoy. It's what he would have wanted. Please, no overeating while reading it. Neither Oprah nor Tolstoy would like it.

The Russian classics are, admittedly, not the most obvious place to look for tips for a happier life. Russian literature is full of gloomy people wondering how on earth they have ended up in the appalling predicament in which they find themselves, looking around desperately for someone else to blame and then realizing that, in fact, they were right in the first place: life really is extremely inconvenient and annoying, and we are all just waiting to die. But they also teach us that it can, crucially, be survived. And it can be enjoyed, beautifully. While Tolstoy looked for answers in his time in didactic philosophy and religious texts, many of us seek comfort in reading about the lives of others, whether in fiction or non-fiction. The pithy sayings in *The Calendar of Wisdom* are useful, inspiring and sometimes even life-changing, but it is great works of literature that really change us as people, by showing us the inner lives of others and by revealing our common humanity. These works allow us to imagine different versions of ourselves, only without having to kill any old ladies (*Crime and Punishment*), have a friendly conversation with Satan on a park bench (*The Master and Margarita*) or throw ourselves under trains (*Anna Karenina*). Warning: there might be a few spoilers in this book, which is surely to be forgiven when most of these works have been around for well over a hundred years.

It's no surprise that Tolstoy himself didn't use fiction as a basis for the advice in his self-help book. We can't expect Tolstoy to admit the usefulness of novels. In the latter part of his life, he had a huge spiritual crisis and all but renounced *Anna Karenina* and *War and Peace* as the writings of a sinful, frivolous fool. No wonder he turned to the Bible. But I want to argue the opposite of what Tolstoy came to believe. Philosophy and religious writings may have their place. And self-help aphorisms from the Greeks always bring solace. But it is in literature – whether novels, plays or poetry – that we really see who we are – and, perhaps even more importantly, who we don't want to be.

But, first, an important disclaimer. This is not an intellectual book. It is not a work of primary research. It is not an academic thesis on Russian literature. It's not supposed to be the last word in interpreting Russian literature. There will be no footnotes, although I've tried to make it as clear as possible where I'm quoting from, and there's a detailed reading list at the back of the book. Instead it's a guide to surviving life using some of the clues left in these great classics. It's an exploration of the answers these writers found to life's questions, big and small. And it's a love letter to some favourite books which at one point helped me to find my identity and buoyed me up when I lost it again. It's also about the times in life when you behave like an idiot, which, for some reason, for me have been remarkably frequent and don't seem to be getting less so as I grow older.

Russian literature deserves more love letters written by total idiots. For too long it has belonged to very clever people who want to keep it to themselves. It's just not true that in order to read the Russian classics you have to be part of some kind of secret society of special people. You definitely don't have to know any Russian or have any plans to ever learn Russian, even though, with me, it was an obsession with studying Russian that pushed me towards these books. You don't even need to know any Russian history, although you will certainly pick up a lot of it in passing. And you don't have to fuss about whether you've got the right translation. Or whether you're missing the entire point. Or whether you need to be sitting next to a samovar. It's accessible to all of us.

I have two university degrees in Russian, and I spent a long time acquiring fluent Russian, using a combination of iron discipline and bison grass vodka. But even after all this, I am no expert. I am a shambling amateur who wants to encourage other shambling amateurs. These books have brought a lot of joy and hope to me, which is something I would never have expected and which endlessly surprises me, as I grew up in a house where we were very much not the sort of people who sat around saying, 'But don't you think Nikolai would have been better off with Sonya in *War and Peace*?' (Frankly, who would want to live in that household?) What I have learned about the Russians is that there is no need to be afraid of them. And there is certainly no need for them to be seen as uniquely 'serious' and 'academic', which we all know are synonyms for 'dusty' and 'boring'.

It's time to take all the doubt and fuss and snobbery and pretence out of this kind of reading. This book is a celebration of the art of reading on its own terms, which is always the most personal thing, and about giving yourself licence to read how you want to read, without feeling that there's always someone else who knows more than you and that maybe you don't really get it. However you get it, you've got it right. I say: read these classics in part if you can't face the whole thing. Don't be afraid not to finish or to come back years later. Read them slowly, without stressing over whether you're understanding every detail. Read them in bed, read them on the bus, read them in the place that Vladimir Putin would call 'the outhouse'. (He once gave a memorable speech in which he assured his people that Russia's enemies were not safe anywhere, even in the outhouse. Please find yourself the safest possible outhouse, which Putin cannot know about, and treat yourself to a few pages of *Three Sisters*.)

As well as shedding some light on some of life's most difficult moments by using examples from these eleven classic Russian works, I'll be looking at some examples from the lives of the writers who wrote them, too. Frequently, there's a mismatch between what the authors seem to advocate in their books and what was going on in their lives. Tolstoy is the classic example. Many of the contradictions, nuances and intricacies of *Anna Karenina* and *War and Peace* can be explained by Tolstoy's later spiritual collapse. When he wrote these books, he empathized hugely with his characters and showed the truth of their lives and feelings. Later on, he felt torn about whether this was a good use of his time and stopped writing those kinds of novels. To know that he was conflicted makes these books even richer with meaning.

The gap between the life of the author, the life of the reader and the text itself has always puzzled me. The thing the reader and the writer have in common is that they're both real and they're both living the life of a human being. They know how difficult life can be. And they know it's almost impossible to express human experience accurately, vividly and believably. However, these two people meet each other on the page, thanks to the story. The story is the stand-in for human experience. It's pretend, it's make-believe. The contract between the writer and the reader says that the writer must agree to make the reader believe in this made-up story. And it's through this agreement that those two people have a meeting of minds and 'discuss' human existence. This is an extraordinary contract, and it's one that is particularly deep in Russian literature.

I'm interested in what these books can teach us about life without us actually having to live through the things described in them. Novels are a way of trying on other people's lives, judging, forgiving, understanding them. They are as good at showing us how not to live as they are at showing us how to live. In fact, they're often better at the former. As many critics have noted, the first line of *Anna Karenina* is intensely memorable and reads beautifully. But the truth of it is not really proved in the novel: 'All happy families are alike; each unhappy family is unhappy in its own way.' In the novel itself, there are no happy families. If Tolstoy wanted to show us one, he could have done. But he doesn't. Instead, he shows us a host of unhappy families, who, ironically enough, do often share things in common: the inability to communicate, the feeling of always thinking that someone else has something better than you, the idea that there must be more to life than this. If anything, Tolstoy's lesson is this: 'How Not to Live'. These are sometimes cautionary tales rather than manuals for living. Maybe that's more real and memorable and therefore more useful than any self-help manual.

Because life is not simple and Russian literature is definitely not simple, there are several outliers in the list of eleven classics featured here. Several don't count as novels. Pushkin's *Eugene*

Onegin is a novel in verse form; Akhmatova's *Requiem* is a set of ten poems; Chekhov's *Three Sisters* is a play, as is Turgenev's *A Month in the Country*. Gogol might even argue that *Dead Souls* is an epic poem. (It isn't really. It's clearly a novel.) So, while this is a book mostly about fictional worlds, it's more precisely about classics of their time and what they have to teach us about life for all time.

There are many books that could have had a place in this list. But I have had to leave out a lot of great works (Dostoevsky's *The Brothers Karamazov*, Lermontov's *A Hero of Our Time*, Marina Tsvetaeva's poetry) in order to avoid this book being as long as *War and Peace* itself. Apologies to Russophiles whose favourites are not present. Of all the books I most wish were here, one is certainly Gogol's *The Overcoat*. For me, this is a short story the plot of which sums up Russian literature in a nutshell. It's about an insignificant copying clerk who saves up for an overcoat. He saves up for a long time. A very long time. On the day the overcoat finally comes into his possession, it is stolen from him. Shortly afterwards, he falls ill and dies. That is Russian literature's idea of a life lesson. You have been warned.

A Note on Sources, Translation, Transliteration and Those Funny Russian Names

However much anyone loves Russian literature, it's easy to see that, generally speaking, from the outside, it is hugely off-putting. First, there's the issue of translation. How do you know which translation to choose? If you're struggling to get through a book, is it the fault of the author or of the translator? Or – God forbid! – of you, the reader? And in any case, even if it is a very good translation, isn't every translation a betrayal of the original? What if it's too good a translation and all the original meaning has been stripped out and anglicized? You'll never read it like a Russian would read it, so what's the point?

These are the kinds of arguments that usually go through someone's mind when approaching the entity people used to call 'the Russians' (meaning 'the great Russian classics'). They're the reason there's a photograph which surfaces on the internet from time to time which depicts a bookshelf proudly showcasing a much-loved copy of *Anna Karenina*. Squashed between other books on the shelf, the spine of the book is bent out of shape an eighth of the way across. The rest of it is pristine and untouched. The picture says it all. This is a book lots of people start (and restart, often many times) but not everyone finishes. But it's also a book no one ever quite gives up on. It's still sitting there, hopefully, on the shelf, waiting for someone to get past the first hundred pages. We all have books like that, books whose spine we hope to crack all the way across one day.

The reputation that accompanies 'the Russians' is fearsome. 'They're deep.' 'They're difficult.' 'They're self-contradicting.' 'You'll never understand X if you haven't read Y.' And on and

9

on. I hate this kind of talk and find it reductive and insular. All literature should be for everyone, no matter how obscure and no matter how supposedly imperfect the translation. When it comes to translation, although I do love long-suffering translators everywhere and see them as the unsung heroes of the modern world, I am not a translation nerd and I don't insist on special favourites. I tend to think that if someone has spent the best part of four or five years translating *War and Peace* (and has been paid by a publisher to do so), they've probably done a pretty good job and there's no point in splitting hairs about whether someone else's job is marginally better. So I just tend to go for the editions of the book that seem to be the most popular or the most recent. I think life is too short to get any more specialized than that. That said, I've tried to pick editions of the books in question here which are easy to get hold of and are generally accepted by people who care deeply about these things as the most readable – or 'best' – translations.

I do sympathize with people's strongly held feelings about translation. As Anthony Briggs writes in his foreword to his translation of *War and Peace*, over time, colloquial language changes and things that once seemed normal suddenly read oddly. Personally, I find this rather charming and wouldn't seek to eliminate it. But Briggs makes the point that in a decent translation you try to get rid of any howlers: 'Infelicities will be edited out, such as "Andrei spent the evening with a few gay friends", "Natasha went about the house flushing", "he exposed himself on the parade ground" or "he ejaculated with a grimace"; we cannot read phrases like these without raising an inappropriate smile.' Ah, but we want some inappropriate smiles! Nonetheless I get it. I get it. No gay privates allowed on parade.

It's as well to assume when reading this book that I am talking about (and quoting from) the translations of the books referred to in the Recommended Reading list at the back. I did my undergraduate degree in Russian in the early 1990s and a postgrad degree ten years later. Back then, I could breeze through a book about Soviet constructivism in Russian, just for fun. (Admittedly, it was about as much fun as it sounds.) So, at some point or another, I have read most of these books in the original language. And where I haven't read them entirely in the original, I have tried bloody hard to give it a go. But a lot of this reading was when I lived in Russia for a year twenty years ago. Nowadays, I don't sit around reading *War and Peace* in Russian. I could have created a huge challenge for myself, gone to live in a cave with some large dictionaries and based everything here on my own translations from the originals. But I thought that would undermine the point I most want to make: that these books are for everyone, not just the special few who have mastered the language. Plus, I love reading literature in translation. You read differently in your own language. I don't think you ever read quite as naturally in another language, no matter how well you acquire it. This is a long-winded way of saying: very few of the translations in this book are mine. (Although if something has been translated wrongly, it's almost definitely me.)

The transliteration in this book is also not mine. Transliteration is a tiresome but necessary phenomenon that I did not come across until I learned Russian. It is the business of transposing Russian (the Cyrillic alphabet) into English (the Latin alphabet). Where I've quoted from a book, both the translation of the Russian and the transliteration of any Russian words come from the editions mentioned in the Recommended Reading. If I have saved myself years of research by not translating anything myself, I have possibly saved even more by not doing the transliterating. I especially hate transliterating.

Over the years, different systems of transliteration have emerged, which is why you sometimes see Chekhov written as 'Tchekov' or Dostoevsky written as 'Dostoyevskii'. None of these different spellings is inherently wrong, but there's an accepted system of transliteration and you are supposed to follow it. Russian and English have many letters and sounds in common. But they also have letters that are incompatible. So, for example, there are single letters in the Russian alphabet for the sound 'ch' and the sound 'shch'. (Yes, these are different sounds.) There is a variation on the letter T (and other consonants) which involves softening that letter with a 'soft sign', represented by an apostrophe in transliteration. And there are several extra vowels in Russian, including a vowel that we don't have in English that is pronounced 'you' and a vowel sound we don't have that is pronounced as something between 'ee' and 'oi'. I can see why you need an agreed system. But I have never been able to master it. So, if there are any transliteration mistakes, they're all mine, too.

Finally, on top of the competing translations, the confusing transliterations and all those feelings of intellectual insecurity which swirl around any time we talk about Russian literature, there is the undeniable business of the names. I once met a Danish academic who was incredibly intelligent and well read and had himself, in one of his books, prescribed reading *War and Peace* for the purposes of intense relaxation. When I praised him for this excellent recommendation, he adopted a pained expression and said, 'Ah, yes, Russian literature is wonderful. But the names! The names! Why do they all have to have forty-seven names?'

He's right, of course, although usually for a character to have more than three or four names would be unusual. It just feels like forty-seven. What derails non-Russians is the use of the patronymic, by which I mean the second bit of Ivan Ivanovich. Really, though, this is very easy to understand, and the more you read patronymics, the more you get used to them and learn to ignore them, as they're not really that useful. In spoken speech, it's polite to use them, but they're almost thrown away and half swallowed.

All 'Ivanovich' is doing is telling you the name of that person's father. Let's say this person is called (and it is entirely plausible) Ivan Ivanovich Ivanov. That means, in Western terms, his name is Ivan Ivanov (Christian name and surname). The 'Ivanovich' bit can more or less be overlooked: it just means that his father's name was also Ivan. Literally, it means: John, Son of John, Of the John Family. In Russian, though, you would never ignore the Ivanovich bit, as it is used as a mark of respect. Instead of saying, 'Hello, Mr Ivanov,' which is what we might say in English to convey respect (instead of saying, 'Hello, Ivan'), Russians would say, 'Hello, Ivan Ivanovich.' ('Hello, John, Son of John.') The words for 'sir' and 'Mister', 'Miss' and 'Mrs' are not commonly used in Russian. They don't need them, because they have the patronymic. It's actually much nicer. (Although quite stressful if you cannot remember someone's patronymic. And by the time you have figured out how to ask subtly, 'By the way, what was your father's name?', you will already have been rude by not addressing them by name, which is a bad thing to do in Russian.)

For women, the rules are the same (the patronymic still refers to their father), only their patronymic will end in, for example, '–evna' or '–ovna' instead of '–evich' or '–ovich'. 'Anna Ivanovna Ivanova.' (Anna, Daughter of John, Of the John Family.) The surname is also changed, to reflect that it's a woman's name. Naturally, this would not be Russian if everyone agreed with this system. So, some people when they are translating from Russian into English do not preserve the difference between the male and female surname. In the edition I've used here, Anna Karenina is Anna Karenina (her patronymic is Arkadyevna because her father's name is Arkady) and her husband is Karenin, with no 'a'. (He is Alexei Alexandrovich, as his father is Alexander. Isn't this fun, guys?)

Some people (let's call them pedants, because that's what they are) get so overexcited about this business of names and transliteration that they fuse the two and become ultra-pernickety. Nabokov, for example, was legendarily testy on this question and refused to accept the idea that it was normal in English to say 'Anna Karenina'. He, without exception, referred to the novel as 'Anna Karenin'. Amusingly, his wife did not agree with his system and always called herself 'Vera Nabokova'. I would like to have been a fly on the wall of the suite of their luxury Swiss hotel when they were discussing this point of difference.

To be fair, it is really easy to see why people get intimidated by all things Russian when you have all this to contend with before you have even started reading a novel. Plus, the patronymic thing is just the beginning. I know what the Danish academic would say now. 'Why, then, is Ivan Ivanovich Ivanov sometimes called Vanya? Is his name Ivan? Or is his name Vanya? Why can't they make up their minds?' 'Vanya' is the diminutive of Ivan. (Like 'Johnny' for John.) But then, of course, you get into the endearments for Ivan: Vanyusha, Vanechka, Vanyushechka, Vanyushka, Ivanyushka . . . (I promise I'm not making this up.) And if you want to be mean, vulgar or jokey, the pejoratives: Vanka, Ivashka. So that's already eleven names for one person. It's not forty-seven, but it's still a lot. Also, every name has these possibilities. For Anna, for example, you could have any of these: Anya, Annochka, Anechka, Nyura, Annushka, Annusha, Annyusya, Anyusha, Annyunya, Nyunya, Nyuta, Anyusya . . . And this doesn't even take into consideration the really silly ones that your family members could make up for fun.

I understand why this is annoying and confusing. I have studied Russian for over two decades, and I still encounter diminutives and can't figure out what name they come from. How you make

Olga into Lyolya or Lyalya is beyond me but, apparently, you do. Dimitry becomes Dima or Mitya or many other things. For Vladimir: Volodya, Vova, Vovochka, Vladik . . . It goes on. I have concluded that it is best not to get hung up on these things and to muddle through as best you can.

The Holy Grail of Russian-speaking is getting so good at it that you feel comfortable making up your own diminutives and still manage to sound authentic. This is how some Russian-speaking friends have ended up calling me mad things like Vivushka and Vivinka. If you're ever lucky enough to be christened with a name like this, my advice is that it's best not to fight it. Equally, if you're encountering names you don't recognize in a Russian novel and it is driving you crazy and making you scream, 'Who the hell is Kolya?' (it's from 'Nikolai' – see also: Kolyenka, Kolka, Kolyan, Lado, Nika, Nikolasha, Nikolenka, Nikolka, Nikusya . . .), try and channel the advice Tolstoy gives in his *Calendar of Wisdom* on 21 October: 'You can't always remain calm, but whenever there are times of peace and calm in your life, you need to value them and try to prolong them.' In other words: don't sweat the diminutives.

One small mercy in Russian literature is that you rarely get the sort of name you hear a lot in everyday spoken Russian. One lovely thing people do when calling names out in everyday life is to give up on all these things completely and just use the first syllable of the name. So, for Alexandra (Sasha), they will just say 'Sash'. For Ivan (Vanya), 'Van'. This is much more like Dave and Bob and Pete. Really, they are just like us. No, really they are. They just have more names for each other.

1. How to Know Who You Really Are: *Anna Karenina* by Lev Tolstoy

(Or: *Don't throw yourself under a train*)

'All the charm, all the beauty and all the diversity
of life are made up of light and shade.'

I came across *Anna Karenina* when I was in my early teens. It coincided with a time in my life when I was becoming desperate to know more about my origins. As a child, I do not remember a time when I thought that my name was anything other than profoundly weird, unexplained and, ultimately, unexplainable. To come across people with similarly odd names was, to me, deeply comforting. I was never put off by the strangeness of the names in Russian literature. They felt familiar. I felt solidarity with them. I did not mind that I couldn't say them aloud with any confidence because I had grown up not speaking any language other than English. But I had, however, lived with an unpronounceable name, and I knew it was not that big a deal, even if other people said it was. 'Viv Groskop. What kind of name is that?'

Growing up in Somerset in the south-west of England, I come from a family that considers itself ordinary, normal and British. Definitely British. I was told this repeatedly as a child. There was nothing in our family history to suggest we were remotely foreign. My grandad was born in Barry, in South Wales. My grandmother was born in Manchester. My dad was from London. My mother and all her family were from Northern Ireland. No one was born abroad. Did I mention there were no foreigners in our family? My great-grandparents on my mother's side were all from Northern Ireland. On my father's side, they were born in Wales or the north of England. As a young child, I knew some of my great-grandparents. There were no foreigners. As you can see, I think I have made it clear that there were no foreigners in our family.

Everything we did was British. Or English. Best not to ask the difference between the two. Mostly British, as my grandad liked to emphasize his Welshness on occasion. And no one wanted to make my mum, born in County Antrim, feel left out. I spent a lot of time with my (paternal) grandparents as a child. My grandad, a grocer for thirty years, had a pathological dislike of all things foreign, especially food. Things like lasagne, minestrone and garlic were 'foreign muck'. Favourite foods in our house were the sorts of foods you would worship if you were the owner of a grocery shop that prided itself on its selection of processed foods: Angel Delight, Bird's Custard, tinned marrowfat peas. These were much safer than foreign muck.

The only thing to disrupt this picture of canned, processed, unquestionable Britishness was the small matter of our name – to me, quite a puzzle: to be undeniably British and yet be called Groskop. Early on, it struck me that something didn't quite add up. This was even before I found out that most of my grandfather's family had changed the spelling of their name from Groskop to 'Groscop'. Now, we were the only people called Groskop. Another mystery. You are not fooling anyone, Groscops, I would think to myself, careful to change the spelling when I was addressing Christmas cards to elderly relatives, at the same time thinking how odd it was.

The Groscops' cunning disguise always struck me as rather desperate. They had changed their name from something foreign-sounding but plausible to something foreign-sounding and implausible. Meanwhile, we, the Groskops, bore the title with some quiet measure of pride – we hadn't sold out and become Groscops! – but, seemingly, zero curiosity.

My family had no sensible answers about the origin of our name. My grandad would talk about it, if pressed, from time to time, only so that we could tease him about the name 'definitely not being German'. He was in the Royal Air Force during the Second World War and was happy for the name to come from anywhere at all on the face of the earth so long as it was not Germany. I soon gravitated towards languages at school and quickly worked out that he was right: it couldn't be German. We would be Grosskopf. ('Bighead.') And we were not Grosskopf. This, at least, I decided, was some mercy. Then Dutch was mentioned as a possibility. But again, the spelling didn't seem right. There was even a crazy idea that we were South African. The name came from Afrikaans, supposedly similar to Dutch. I struggled to believe this.

The lack of information made me obsessive about origins and names. When I was four years old, we acquired a cat, a cute little tortoiseshell thing. I was allowed to name her. I called her Jane. She brought me a lot of comfort, even though I later became aware that I had saddled the cat with a feline name just as unlikely for her as my human name was for me. (Who calls a cat Jane?) For years, I dreamed of having the surname Smith. This to me was a wonderful, beautiful name, one no one would ever mispronounce or spell incorrectly. And no one would ever ask where you came from.

It wasn't until I was about twelve or thirteen that I picked up a copy of *Anna Karenina*. I got it in a charity shop, I think, in the mid-1980s. It was an old Penguin Classic. The cover features the painting that has come to be the most frequent stand-in for Anna Karenina: Ivan Kramskoi's *Portrait of an Unknown Woman* of 1883. I loved that picture, but the name sold the novel to me first. Karenina. A name that is simple and yet one that people hesitate to pronounce. I knew some people said it as 'Carry

Nina', but you should say it 'Kar-ray-ni-na', with the emphasis on the 'ray'. I fell in love with her name. And then I fell in love with her face. The moment I saw this stunning woman, all velvet coat, alabaster skin, fur-trimmed beret and air of mystery, my spotty, chubby, insecure adolescent self thought: 'This is the me I have been looking for. Definitely not German, Dutch or South African. But why not Russian?' It was a half-thought that was to change the course of my life.

The identity of the model in the Kramskoi painting is unknown and, to protect the blushes of my twelve-year-old self, we will overlook the fact that she was most likely a prostitute. Although Kramskoi never said the woman was meant to be Anna Karenina, it's entirely possible that he read the novel and had her in mind when he painted the portrait, whether consciously or not. He had painted Tolstoy in 1873, when the novelist was just starting to write the novel. We can't know for sure, though, that this is her. Nevertheless, it says a lot that many people have wanted to see Anna Karenina in this picture. We want the Unknown Woman to be real. Especially those of us who have wanted to be her.

This isn't a great ambition, incidentally, as it is doomed to failure. On first reading, I became obsessed with the thickness of Anna Karenina's eyelashes. Tolstoy loves the details of women's faces. He writes of Anna having eyelashes so thick that they make her grey eyes look darker. Inspired by this bewitching beauty, I started using an eyelash curler to achieve a similar effect. If you've never seen an eyelash curler, it's like a miniature medieval torture instrument and must be employed with great care and skill. One day, I got a bit distracted and sneezed while using it. I had pulled out all my eyelashes on one side, giving me a naked eyelid and a lopsided squint. It took about a year for them to grow back. Much later on, I discovered that, in an earlier draft, Tolstoy had given Anna Karenina a hairy upper lip.

That would have been easier for me to work with, and a lot less painful than the accidental eyelash removal. Liza in *War and Peace* also has a moustache. Clearly, Tolstoy had a fetish.

The desire to identify with Anna Karenina as a character – to believe her to be 'real', to believe her to be 'us' – is understandable. It's one of the most attractive things about the novel. Although, on the surface of things, *Anna Karenina* seems to be a morality tale about a doomed, beautiful but adulterous romance, really this is a book about identity, integrity and our purpose in life. Who are we and why are we here? These questions are deeply embedded in it. They are questions that tortured Tolstoy and, almost as soon as he had published *Anna Karenina*, they caused him to renounce his work and retreat into himself. It's partly this feeling of crisis that has made me feel bound to this novel my whole life. It's a fantastic meditation on identity and what we're doing here. But it doesn't really answer any questions. To such an extent that it's enough to drive you mad. In fact, it almost drove Tolstoy to suicide.

However, it's easy to read *Anna Karenina* without becoming a tortured religious maniac. Because it is a cracking story. Anna Arkadyevna Karenina is the wife of Alexei Alexandrovich Karenin, a government minister. She is a woman in her mid to late twenties. Her husband is two decades older. She is bored and disillusioned with her life. She finds herself drawn to an extremely attractive young officer called Vronsky, who is not a particularly unpleasant person but does not have much more than his looks to recommend him. Their love affair is passionate and tender but, ultimately, Anna cannot enjoy it because she feels guilty, not so much because of her irritating husband, Karenin, but because of her maternal responsibilities to her young son, Seryozha, whom she loves very much. (Diminutive alert: Seryozha is short for Sergei.) In the moment that she resolves to divorce Karenin and risk no longer being a part of her child's life, she loses her nerve and disappears under the wheels of a train. Bad times.

In the course of the novel, Tolstoy weaves the parallel tale of Levin, a principled, intellectual young man whose character is — surprise, surprise! — not unlike that of our esteemed author (who, at the time of writing, has already had success with *War and Peace* and is no stranger to Great Literature). Levin is a friend of Anna's brother Stiva. There's another link, too: Stiva's sister-in-law Kitty has attracted the attentions of both Levin and Vronsky (initially, before he becomes involved with Anna). Levin's emerging relationship with Kitty, one that represents contentment and peace but also (potentially) boredom and predictability, serves as a point of comparison for the romance between Vronsky and Anna, whose union symbolizes anxiety and the breaking of trust but also excitement and risk. This parallel between the two couples is something that is not often noted but it is crucial in understanding the point Tolstoy is making about the nuances of happiness and knowing who we are. Without Anna's seduction of Vronsky (or vice versa), Kitty might not have been free to go off with Levin. One person's happiness is often dependent on the unhappiness of another. And what we think of as unhappiness may ultimately lead to happiness. (Kitty is not supposed to end up with Vronsky. They would not have been good together.)

On the surface, *Anna Karenina* is about relationships and, more importantly, about the perils of infidelity. But Tolstoy messes up his own message by falling in love with Anna Karenina and by making her supposedly 'unhappy' life more ambiguous than perhaps he had intended. There's a moralistic thread running through the book, certainly. And Anna Karenina herself receives the most severe punishment. But the way Tolstoy writes about her, you can sense that he sympathizes with her. The lesson in the novel is that we must try to know who we really are in order to live an authentic life. Anna realizes that her life with Vronsky is authentic but unachievable, and feels she has no option but to kill herself. If you wanted to read something revolutionary into the novel, that is definitely an option. Instead of a comment on how 'wrong' Anna is, her death could represent a judgement on the morals of the society of the time. 'Look what you've made her do, when her only crime was to fall in love and be who she really is.' If anything, the message Tolstoy imparts in *Anna Karenina* is a compromised one. Levin's way of life seems the 'correct' one. And yet it is Anna who appears to be truly alive, even though she is ultimately doomed to punishment.

It is not surprising that *Anna Karenina* is frequently described as the greatest novel of all time, precisely because of the way it approaches these big questions but without finding easy answers. William Faulkner held this view, as did Dostoevsky. Nabokov – who was an incredibly grumpy person and did not suffer fools gladly (even less so than Dostoevsky, which is really saying something) – said the style was 'flawless magic'. Tolstoy himself considered it a better novel than *War and Peace*. In fact, he did not even consider *War and Peace* to be a novel. He thought it was episodic fiction, a series of short stories. *Anna Karenina*, however, was a novel and – initially – he thought it was good. I often wonder what Sofya, Tolstoy's wife, thought about him considering the 2,200-page *War and Peace* 'not a novel'. She had to copy it out repeatedly. I imagine she had some other words to describe it, and probably quite diminutive words at that.

Of course, there are many answers in the novel to the question 'How should you live your life?' You could choose a simple, unquestioning life of luxury like Anna's brother Stiva, a man who only drinks champagne with people he likes (and he drinks champagne with everyone). Or you could choose Levin's path: self-sacrificing, righteous, spiritual. Levin is supposed to be the prototype for happiness – for example, with his steady, even rhythm of life – but he doesn't in fact seem that happy and frequently tortures himself about whether he should be spending more time ploughing fields.

There is an intriguing mix of hedonism and self-flagellation in *Anna Karenina*. Before the author, in the early chapters, has even invited us to the Anglia Hotel for a slap-up meal of oysters and turbot with Stiva (Anna's brother) and Levin, Stiva's best friend, Tolstoy has already casually dropped in the Epigraph of Doom: 'Vengeance is mine. And I will repay.' It's a quotation that suggests that, in life, if there is any revenge to be taken, God will sort it out in his own way. You had better not do it yourself. It is an incredibly powerful and disturbing choice of words to slap on the page next to the title of your novel, and one that marks Tolstoy out as someone who is obsessed – or beginning to be obsessed – with God and with the idea that it is foolish to imagine we are in charge of our lives (because we're not in charge, God is). It sounds very much like the voice of God himself. And it doesn't exactly mark Tolstoy out as Mr Fun Times.

The heavy-handed, preachy tone of that scary epigraph is a harbinger of the sort of writing Tolstoy was to specialize in later in life, after he more or less disowned *Anna Karenina*. Even at the time he was writing the novel, he was already tortured by a lot of the philosophical ideas that came to dominate his thinking and led him to a monk-like existence as a teetotal vegetarian, committed consumer of boiled eggs and serial avoider of pastries. (So often, I've wanted to travel back in time and get him to try a jam doughnut. I feel sure he would have written more novels. The man just needed sugary carbohydrates.)

But it's also a strange lesson in wishful thinking. I can't help feeling that Tolstoy wanted God to take his revenge on Anna Karenina (for being a dirty, filthy adulteress) but, at the same time, the human being in him (who had committed a lot of dirty, filthy adultery himself) sees her fragility and attractiveness as a person and wants to forgive her. The contradictory nature of the epigraph is a clue as to why *Anna Karenina* is such a complicated novel and does not deliver a clear, unambiguous message about how to live. On the one hand, Tolstoy sets out to write a didactic novel where no one dares challenge God's laws without terrible consequences and where Levin (the 'good' Tolstoy) is the hero of the piece. And yet, on the other hand, and almost in spite of himself, he ends up drawing a beautiful portrait of Anna Karenina, infused with empathy and compassion. There's a way of looking at Anna not just as a character and a woman but as an extension of Tolstoy himself: the 'bad' Tolstoy, the foolish side of himself that he wishes didn't exist.

It's this contradiction that makes Tolstoy the best guide to life. He is both flawed and honest, and these qualities are not always intentional. In fact, he tries to cover them up. But that only makes him more likeable. Even the most cursory glance at his life shows that he was an immensely and amusingly complex character. That is why – with reservations – I love him. He is a tricky bugger, with many bad character traits and psychological inconsistencies, which plagued him his whole life and which he tried desperately to overcome. But aren't these very much the qualities anyone should seek in a lifelong friend?

Everything you need to know about Tolstoy is summed up by what he did to his wife on the eve of their wedding. He was thirty-four. She was seventeen. He felt bad about the fact that he had had a debauched youth, sleeping with prostitutes, Gypsies and parlourmaids. He had fathered a child by one of the serfs on the estate. (I love that in the author biography in the original Penguin edition of *Anna Karenina* this is described as 'a life of pleasure'. It's what my grandma would call the life of Riley.) He felt so bad about all these 'pleasures' that he showed his wife-to-be his diaries, which extensively detailed all his exploits and the venereal disease they had resulted in. The same episode plays out, of course, between Levin and Kitty in *Anna Karenina*. Decades later, in her diaries, his wife wrote that she never recovered from the shock.

This information about Tolstoy's character has always been out there and has been easy to find if you were looking for it. However, in the past decade in Russia, there has been a resurgence of interest in Tolstoy the real person (as opposed to Tolstoy the great genius) thanks to *Flight from Paradise*, a fascinating biography by Pavel Basinsky. This book is a controversial account of Tolstoy's final days and won Russia's national book prize. Until recently in Russia, and since the dawn of time in academia, looking too deeply into a writer's biography has been frowned upon, because this is seen to lead to a shallow appreciation of the important thing: the writing. But something about Basinsky's book broke the spell for Russians, and everyone became fixated by it. An entire nation thought to themselves: 'What if we looked at Tolstoy as an ordinary person who struggled with his emotions, got very angry with his wife and had very particular feelings about serving suggestions for eggs?' This was the Tolstoy Basinsky uncovered, and Russians loved it. I have no evidence that egg sales from Arkhangelsk to Vladivostok soared, but I like to pretend to myself that they did.

Here was a man who was difficult, infuriating, sometimes rather cruel to his family and tortured by his own nature. This, at least, explained a lot of the contradictions and complexities in his work, including why the themes in *Anna Karenina* can be so hard to pin down. Basinsky's book also sought to give some context to what is perhaps the most shocking act of self-loathing in literary history. Almost as soon as Tolstoy finished the novel, he renounced all artistic work in favour of what he called a 'spiritual rebirth'. As discussed, I know we are not supposed to read too much into authors' biographies. But I really don't think you can ignore the fact that someone writes a novel full of emotion and passion which becomes known as one of the greatest works of art ever created and then they turn around and basically say, 'Well, that was a disgusting waste of time. I am going to go and be a peace-loving vegetarian now.'

If anything, Tolstoy's new reputation as a more rounded person who ate boiled pears to aid his digestion (no wonder, with all the eggs) – rather than some kind of literary demigod – has enhanced the understanding and appreciation of his work. I certainly feel better for knowing that the eighty-two-year-old Tolstoy went around wearing two hats because he felt the cold on his head, that he loved beans and Brussels sprouts (a rare break from the eggs) and that, on one occasion, his wife was so angry with him for leaving the house without telling her that she stabbed herself with knives, scissors and a safety pin. (Theirs was an extraordinarily volatile relationship, especially in later life, and it was exacerbated – understandably – by Tolstoy's desire to renounce the works that supported the family financially. Not to mention Sofya Andreyevna's role as Chief Copier-Outer of the novels.)

In *Flight from Paradise*, Basinky also revealed Tolstoy to be someone suffering from a lot of problems we would judge as uniquely modern. Whenever any of us reads about someone being hassled on social media and what a contemporary phenomenon this is considered to be, we should think about Tolstoy. He routinely received death threats via telegram, letter and parcel. On his eightieth birthday in 1908, he received a large box containing a length of rope. It's all very well someone sending you a poison-pen letter. But a length of rope? That is hardcore. The letter accompanying the rope was signed 'A mother'. His wife, Sofya, opened it and wrote in her diary that the message with it read: 'There is nothing left for Tolstoy to do but wait for and wish for the government to hang him, and he can save them the trouble.' Sofya noted that she assumed the woman had lost a child in the revolution in 1905 and blamed Tolstoy for it.

Whenever Tolstoy travelled, he was subject to constant distractions, bombarded by other people's opinions, thoughts and arguments; it was as if a Twitter-come-to-life materialized before him. (Genuine report: 'Can I get your autograph, Lev Nikolayevich? By the way, would you ever go in an aeroplane?' He gave the autograph and said that aeroplanes were a bad idea, as only birds should fly.) At home, it wasn't much better: people continually came to his house (interrupting, at least, the frequent deliveries of rope) to ask for work or money, or to show him their terrible manuscripts. The only way he could get away from them was to go and visit his sister in the monastery where she lived, which was in itself really stressful, because he had been excommunicated by the Church and was not at all welcome there. Poor Tolstoy.

Knowing that Tolstoy suffered all this after he had renounced *Anna Karenina* has helped me to be more patient about trying to understand the book's messages. It is one of the strangest novels, in that it reads so beautifully and easily and is full of light and warmth. And yet, when you sit back and think about its ultimate meaning, it is like the breath of Satan. Its ultimate message? 'Don't want anything too selfish because you will end up killing yourself.' And while the novel has so much soulful joy and gentle humour, and even elements of self-deprecation (especially in Tolstoy's portrait of Levin, the character most like himself), there is an oddness to the book, a disturbing sense of unresolved conflict.

It doesn't help, for example, that the heroine doesn't appear until Chapter Eighteen. When you read this novel for the first time, you also spend a great many pages (sixty or seventy, depending on which edition you're reading) thinking, 'Yes, yes, that's all very well. Some very nice vodka parties and excellent ice skating. But where is – drum roll – Anna Karenina? Isn't this supposed to be a book about her?' The moment when she arrives is almost an anticlimax. It's sudden and brief. Considering this is arguably the greatest heroine in literary history, our first meeting with Anna Karenina is tantalizingly delayed and strangely underwhelming. 'Vronsky followed the conductor to the carriage and at the door to the compartment stopped to allow a lady to leave.' A lady! It is the lady! Has there ever been a more low-key introduction? First, the scary, vengeful epigraph. And now this weird lack of focus on the heroine.

Let's revisit this for a moment. He 'stopped to allow a lady to leave'. That's it? That's her entrance? Really? This is typical Tolstoy. Bring on the most important character seemingly in passing and disturbingly late in the day. Let her emerge out of the background. Don't make a big deal about it. It's a deferred entrance that credits the reader with a lot of intelligence, not to mention the patience of a saint. We immediately sense – without having to be told – that the train lady is Anna. We understand (or at least assume) her significance. But the writer respects us enough not to push her in our faces. He does not want to do us the disservice of announcing: 'Look! It's Anna Karenina! And she's doomed! Doomed, I tell you!' (I can't help feeling that, if this were Dickens, a passing tramp would announce this. No offence, Dickens.) Of course, by doing something so unusual, so bold and so seemingly discreet (blink and you'll miss her), Tolstoy presents his heroine even more ostentatiously than if he'd delivered her bursting out of a train-shaped cake dancing the can-can and singing 'Chattanooga Choo Choo'.

The funny thing is, the whole of the first part of the book is about Stepan Oblonsky – Stiva (yes, it's the diminutive again) or, in some crazy translations which totally disregard all laws of transliteration and common sense, 'Steve' – Anna's brother, a civil servant and man about town. If the first sixty pages of this novel were anything to go by, then it should be called 'Anna Karenina's Brother' or, perhaps, 'The Book of Steve'. Although it's really not a good idea to think of his name being Steve, as these misguided translations suggest. He's really not a Steve. A Steve would not order oysters and turbot and drink champagne with ladies of dubious morals doused in vinaigre de toilette, a nineteenth-century perfume consisting of plants, woods and spices. If this were not *Anna Karenina* and instead 'The Book of Steve' (sorry, Stiva), I guess this would happen on every page. (I know I'm contradicting myself here, by the way, because I said earlier that I am not fussy about names. But, seriously, Stiva Oblonsky is *not* a Steve. This is one occasion where correct transliteration is necessary and warranted.)

Arguably, Oblonsky – who goes to meet Anna off the train, where, during the journey, she has just sat next to Vronsky's mother – is the glue of the whole book. Anna is his sister. Levin is his best friend. Vronsky is his (sort of) work colleague. Stiva is a civil servant and Vronsky is a cavalry officer. They are both members of the aristocracy, and Stiva would make it his business to know everything about everyone in high society. But, of course, this is not a novel about Stepan Oblonsky. It can't be. Because he is a supposedly happy man who has figured life out. It is a novel about Anna Karenina. It has to be. Because she is an unhappy woman who has not got life figured out. Although there's already a contradiction here. We can see that Anna's brother is supposed to be 'the happy one'. And yet we know that his merry and debauched life has led to misery. He's having an affair. His wife knows about it, and she's distraught. He's devastated, in turn, to have upset her. This is why Anna has come to visit: to console her brother's wife and plead his case. And this is supposed to be the version of 'the happy family'. Clearly, we are not meant to take everything at face value.

Neither are we to be distracted by the joyful hedonism of

Stiva's existence, which dominates the early pages of the book. That's far too enjoyable and, in Tolstoy's eyes, shallow. Not long after Tolstoy finished *Anna Karenina*, he wrote in his legendary essay *A Confession* that the meaninglessness of life is 'the only indisputable piece of knowledge available to man'. Oh, Tolstoy, you old grump. He foreshadows this thought, just as he fore-shadows Anna's death, with a classic piece of doom-mongering as soon as we meet her. On the next page, once Anna's beauty, tenderness and inexplicably enigmatic charm have been established, Tolstoy squishes a watchman under the wheels, with some relish. 'Cut in two pieces, they say.' 'Threw himself! . . . Run over! . . .' All right, all right. Don't go on about it. Anna speaks for Tolstoy at this point: '"A bad omen," she said.' You don't say.

This omen is intentional. Tolstoy knew from the beginning of the book that Anna Karenina would die in a train accident at the end, because that is what happened in real life. The year before Tolstoy started the novel, a neighbour of his had an altercation with his mistress. Her name was Anna Stepanovna Pirogova. (Rather brilliantly, her name means something like 'Anna of All the Pies'. Surely this would have been a much better title? Even better than 'The Book of Steve'.) In Henri Troyat's biography of Tolstoy, he recounts that this woman was 'a tall, full-blown woman with a broad face and an easy-going nature'. I feel this may well be code for 'fat' or 'pie-filled'. Anyway. Tolstoy's neighbour had thrown Anna of All the Pies over for a German governess. The real-life Anna (of All the Pies) took it badly, wandered the countryside distraught for three days and then threw herself under a train. (I am so tempted to add: 'There was pie everywhere.' But that would be insensitive.)

Anna Stepanovna Pirogova left a note: 'You are a murderer. Be happy, if an assassin can be happy. If you like, you can see my corpse on the rails at Yasenki.' Tolstoy went to the autopsy, which took place on 5 January 1872. Let's just think for a moment about the sort of person who would do that and how it might have affected him . . . When he began writing *Anna Karenina*, he gave his heroine the dead woman's first name and used her patronymic (Stepanovna) for the name of Anna Karenina's brother, Stepan. I cannot be alone in thinking this is creepy.

So while we, the readers, don't know the fate of Anna Karenina when we first meet her stepping off (gulp) a train, Tolstoy knows all along and plays with us by hinting at what's in store. The first time we see Anna, of all the places Tolstoy could have chosen to reveal her, it just has to be emerging from a train carriage, doesn't it? And, equally naturally and unavoidably, it has to be a train that has just crushed someone to death. In the early pages, the novel builds up to the first glimpse of Anna with beautiful prose and so much suspense. Tolstoy makes you spend ages unwrapping this precious gift, tearing off layer upon layer of narrative describing endless provincial balls and fur coats and taffeta dresses, only to find that the prize, when it finally arrives, is shrouded in smoke and steam, upstaged by the shouts of people who have just seen (and I quote) a 'mangled corpse'.

Tolstoy didn't have to foreshadow her death. But he can't resist warning us that he's not really sure that he has anything more to impart, other than the idea that we are basically doomed. It's as if Tolstoy is saying: 'Yes, I will show you the meaning of life. But first I just have to work it out for myself. In the meantime, read this novel, which may or may not contain some clues.' I'm paraphrasing. Tolstoy would never say this. Instead, he would say something like: 'All the variety, all the charm, all the beauty of life, is made up of light and shade.' It's Stiva, Anna's brother, who says this. (Levin – the Tolstoy of the piece – isn't listening, of course.) Tolstoy can create beauty and magic. But he is like the Wizard of Oz, all smoke and mirrors, and pretending and grandiosity. Underneath it all he is just a man on the brink of a breakdown who wants to eat a lot of eggs.

Anna Karenina, both the character and the novel, embodies the questions Tolstoy spent his whole life trying to answer. What shall I do with this life? What does it mean to live a good life? How will I know I've done the right thing? Is it all arbitrary? Or is there some grand plan for us? If it's all arbitrary, how do we decide what to do within that? And if there's a grand plan, where do we find it written down so that we know to follow it? It's Levin who asks a lot of these questions in *Anna Karenina*. But it's Anna who has to live them out.

There is a grand plan, and Tolstoy wrote it down in his work. Except it isn't a very good plan. It's easy to read his novels and think, 'Wow. Tolstoy does not have a clue about life. All his characters just flounder around, often betraying their friends and occasionally noticing a beautiful sunset.' (As we will discover later, this is basically the plot of *War and Peace*.) But once you have read a lot of him, you start to think, 'Oh. Tolstoy knows a lot about life. He depicts people who are a mess because that's normal, honest and real.' This is both heartening and, at the same time, deeply frustrating.

I often wonder whether part of Tolstoy's struggle with figuring out what we are here for is connected to his relationship with other people. Understanding people was a burden to Tolstoy. He was a solitary character who spent many hours alone, writing. And yet, despite the arguments he had with his family when he was much older, he also loved to be surrounded by his children, read stories to them and chase them around the dinner table. *Anna Karenina* is a testament to how observant he was in everyday family life. He was a man who noticed all the intimate details. He loves to mention his affection for the hair on women's upper lips; he makes fleeting mention of birth control (in a conversation between Dolly, Stiva's wife, and Anna); and he cares about sore nipples after childbirth (Dolly mentions this). He had a longing for connection with other people which was at odds with his intellectual self. I think, rationally, he wanted to be able to judge others, including himself. But he was unable to because he had too much heart and empathy. As he says of the saintly Levin and the hedonistic Oblonsky: 'To each of them it seemed that the life he was leading was the only real life, and the one his friend led was a mere illusion.' You have to be able to understand other people to think like this. If only Tolstoy had extended the kindness that he extended to his characters in his 'frivolous' novel to himself. But, still, this is one of the most charming things about Tolstoy: the gap between the intimidating nature of his reputation and the more reassuring, human facts of his biography.

What, though, about the enduring mystery of the most famous opening line in literary history? 'All happy families are alike; each unhappy family is unhappy in its own way.' Is it just a clever bit of wording? Or is there something deeper about happiness to be found here? It is a great piece of advice, as long as you don't take it too literally. Tolstoy spends eight hundred pages illustrating exactly what he means by it. The traits of a happy life are predictable and constant. In Tolstoy's estimation, they would include having a family life (Tolstoy believed it was important to have children), living productively (whatever this means to you – although Tolstoy would probably think that you should do quite a lot of hoeing as part of this) and being at peace with your lot in life (something Tolstoy himself did not really achieve). Despite being prolific and deeply engaged with his work, he was not a materially ambitious person and, long before *A Calendar of Wisdom*, was always making lists of ways he could improve himself spiritually: 'Each person's task in life is to become an increasingly better person.'

So, while it's easy to predict the common traits that cause happiness, unhappiness is unique, he concludes. The takeaway? We are better off concentrating on the things that have worked for everyone else, rather than concentrating on our individual misery. Copy people who look as if their lives have worked out. Talk to them. Emulate them. Follow them. Don't try to impress people by sleeping around, contracting lots of venereal diseases and then having to tell your bride-to-be about it. This is a compassionate way of looking at life. Don't think too hard about happiness. When it comes, enjoy it. Try not to get fixated on the causes of your unhappiness.

Anna Karenina regrets her suicide while she is in the very act. Just as she is pulled under the wheels, she says, horrified: 'Where am I? What am I doing? Why?' We get it. There's not much point in her asking these questions now. She had her chance. She blew it. Tolstoy's message? We need to make sure we ask these questions. But not quite so late.

In the end, Tolstoy appears to be asking something about literature itself. Is it really the job of novels to tell us how to live? Sadly, in his own life, he came to the conclusion that *Anna Karenina* had showed him how not to live: he did not want to be the person who wrote entertaining, complex novels. In coming to this realization, he failed to follow his own advice and, instead of being like other happy people, he became uniquely unhappy in his own fashion. The final message of *Anna Karenina*? It's all very well looking for answers, but life is, essentially, unknowable. We must search desperately for meaning. Sometimes we will come close to it, but most of the time we will be disappointed and then we will die. Sorry about that. Did I mention that not all the lessons would be cheery? Come on, this is Russian literature we're talking about, after all.

2. How to Face Up to Whatever Life Throws at You: *Doctor Zhivago* by Boris Pasternak

(Or: Don't leave your wife while she's pregnant)

'How wonderful to be alive, he thought.
But why does it always hurt?'

The strange thing about learning a new language is that the more you learn, the more you start to pick up clues about the psychology of the people who speak the language. When I first went to Russia in 1992 and was starting to speak enough Russian to understand what people were saying to me, I was astonished to find that they genuinely spoke about 'fate' the whole time, like something out of a bad Bond film. It was so weird that, initially, I thought I was imagining it or misunderstanding the words. 'Why? You ask why? No reason. It's fate.' 'You are in Russia at an important historical moment. It is your fate.' And often: 'Drink it. It's your fate, Vivka.' Yes, I finally had a group of friends who had gifted me 'Vivka' (Little Viv) as my very own personal diminutive. My elderly landlady once misheard this as 'Veepka' (Little VIP, as the initials VIP are pronounced 'veep' in Russian) so I was also known as that: Vivka, Veep (VIP) or Vipulya (Tiny Little VIP) or Vipulenka (Dearest Teeny Tiny Little VIP). This was all extremely odd, as these names were used completely earnestly and not as a joke. I just got used to people shouting, across a room, 'Dearest Teeny Tiny Little VIP, come over here!'

After a while, I even became unaware of this and thought it was normal. There is so much strangeness to the Russian language that you give up noticing it. Along with 'fate' and being called Dearest Teeny Tiny Little VIP, the concept of 'soul' came up constantly in everyday conversation. The answer to anything difficult to explain? 'It is the Russian soul.' The best kind of music, theatre or writing? 'You can feel it in your soul.' The highest compliment? 'You have a Russian soul.'

People would genuinely say these things in conversation, in passing. And not just people who were a bit odd and ridiculously intense – although a lot of people I met during the early 1990s were both those things. Everyone. Fate and soul are big things for Russians. They feel them. They regard them as intensely real. I was initially sceptical about their existence. But then I realized how useful they are. 'Soul' is perhaps close to what we might call instinct. Ignore it at your peril. 'Fate' is what we call reality. It's good to accept both.

The greatest expression in literature of these twin feelings is Pasternak's epic novel *Doctor Zhivago*. Yury Zhivago has the most Russian of souls, and he does what he can to survive his fate. The novel opens with a funeral scene, as brief as it is depressing. Yuri's mother is being buried. He is ten years old. As the coffin is lowered, the earth scattered and the grave filled, Yuri climbs up on to the mound, raises his head as if he is about to howl like a wolf, and bursts into tears. This is classic Pasternak. Set a scene, decorate it with certain picturesque elements and unleash the feelings. Whenever I think of *Doctor Zhivago*, I think of that funeral scene and of the only Russian funeral I attended. It was the experience I would return to in my memory whenever I thought about my relationship to Russia. I have never felt more foreign at any moment in my life, before or since.

The day I would first experience the Russian idea of 'fate' started ridiculously early, with a dull, distant banging on the door at 5.30 a.m. The sound reached me vaguely, as if I were under water. I was still fast asleep and dreaming strange, feverish dreams. A year after I had been christened Tiny Little VIP during the summer of my first trip to Russia, I returned to St Petersburg for my university year abroad, to teach English and, hopefully, become fluent in Russian. Before leaving, I had watched *The Shining*. This was a terrible mistake. First, I hate horror films and find myself very easily haunted by them in the best of circumstances. Second, the hostel where I was staying, in north-west St Petersburg, looked very much like the guesthouse featured in the film, with its long, poorly lit corridors and flickering overhead lighting. If you were going to kill someone, cover your traces, then write 'Red Rum' on a mirror in Cyrillic, this would have been an extremely good place to do it. I was full of apprehension, anxiety and a sort of terrified awe about living in a place that felt more like a 1970s information film about Communism than a real place. I had sweaty dreams where Jack Nicholson shouted at me in Russian.

The atmosphere was already psychologically charged. So it did not help that no one in charge of our group of a dozen fresh-faced would-be teachers of English seemed to have any idea what was going on. We were told that we would soon be meeting with 'a Methodist'. We had visions of Bibles and prayer books. Our group leader said she had no idea why things suddenly seemed to have taken on a religious dimension, but she didn't like to ask too many questions. It later turned out that the Russian word 'methodist' simply means someone who trains you in teaching methods; it has nothing to do with the Methodist faith of John Wesley. As we awaited further instruction, I navigated the mostly empty local shops, acquiring menthol cigarettes, vast quantities of toilet paper (anticipating a shortage, as it seemed the only thing to be freely available) and a rather beautiful Soviet hand-stitched bra for a very small amount of roubles. Meanwhile, a friend died. Not a close friend. But a friend, nonetheless.

That early-morning knock at the door was not unexpected. Several days earlier, the news had reached me that a young Russian woman I knew had killed herself. She would have been eighteen or nineteen. I was twenty at the time. Masha was not someone I knew intimately, but I considered her a friend and I was fond of her. Out of our group just arrived from the UK, I was one of the few who already had friends in St Petersburg, people I knew from three visits to the city over the previous year. I had first visited Russia the year before, in a last-ditch attempt to understand Russian, having almost failed my exams at the end of my first year at university.

Life was extraordinarily hard for the young Russians I befriended in the early 1990s. And it wasn't easy for them to have me as their friend. I represented something exotic and exciting. For some people, I was, potentially, a source of money or treats or – what everyone really wanted – jeans, ideally Levi's. I once had an awful conversation with one of my students when I was teaching English, when he asked me what I was getting my (Ukrainian) boyfriend for Christmas: 'Jeans,' I replied, without thinking. There was an inevitable pause while we both considered the fact that I probably shouldn't have admitted to this. He shot back meaningfully: 'I could also do with some jeans.' Awkward. I knew that the relationship I had with some of these friends was artificially intimate because of my status as a foreigner. But we liked each other and had some good times together. Still, it was a strange and unbalanced relationship. One thing I was ill equipped for in this context, both linguistically and emotionally, was a death, especially the suicide of someone my own age.

My immediate reaction was shock and sadness for Masha's mother (whom I had met only once) and concern for the other friends who had known her since childhood. One response I had was also fairly pragmatic: 'All their lives are depressing. And

Masha was one of the happy ones. This will give them ideas.' It also struck me, rather unfairly, that this incident was indicative of Russian life. I had gone through British life for two decades without knowing anyone who had committed suicide. I had barely been in Russia two weeks and one of the dozen people I knew had killed herself.

I had mixed feelings about Masha's death, and about attending her funeral. I worried that it would be inappropriate for me to go, as someone who wasn't among her closest friends and as someone who was a foreigner, an outsider. On the other hand, though, I knew that having a foreigner there would probably carry some kind of kudos which would be attractive to her friends and her family, and that there would be other friends who would want me to go. It might be some kind of consolation. Or it might be an imposition. It was impossible to know how to behave. It became obvious that everyone expected me to go and that it would cause offence not to. (Along with 'fate' and 'soul', the concept of causing offence is huge in Russia. The refusal of the tiniest thing can be countered with: 'You are offending me.')

I find it strange that, now, I don't remember exactly what reason was given for Masha's suicide. I remember being obsessed with the question at the time. I was frustrated with my own inability to understand everything that was being said to me in Russian and equally frustrated with my lack of vocabulary to offer alternatives. I distinctly recall someone saying something I did understand: *'Prosto ne khotela bol'she zhit'.'* ('She just didn't want to live any more.') This was accompanied by a shrug that said: 'You know what that's like.' I suppose, as teenagers, we all felt we understood. But, really, we understood nothing. Many years later, I found out that the Belorussian Nobel Prize winner Svetlana Alexievich had written *Enchanted with Death*, a book about the outbreak of suicides in the country around the same time, just after the collapse of the Soviet Union: her explanation was that life became too uncertain and confusing for many people and they just couldn't take it any longer. Also, many felt caught up in the Communist project, and the failure of that ideology symbolized something personal for them. Masha seemed an unlikely candidate for this way of thinking. She was plump and pretty and had a face that was so doll-like it was almost comical. She had cherubic cheeks that made her look like a *matrioshka*, with puffy, brown, curly hair. She was a cheerful girl: friendly, sweet, innocent. I still find it hard to believe that what she did was intentional and not just the proverbial cry for help.

The morning I heard the dull knocking at the door, I had no desire to get up and half-wash myself in a tiny cubicle crawling with cockroaches. The bathroom of the student hostel had tiles which were crumbling off the walls. Insects and Soviet plaster intermingled, and a draught whistled through the cracks. Outside, it was freezing. It was a dry, biting cold, the sort you never quite got used to, even in St Petersburg. Neither did I have any idea what to wear: I had no black clothes and, crucially, no black coat. The only coat I had with me was completely unsuitable for most occasions, and definitely unsuitable for a funeral. It was an old man's brown leather jacket with a sheepskin lining. I had bought it in a second-hand shop and thought it made me look like something out of *Quadrophenia*. In fact, it made me look more like something out of *The Archers*. It was not made to be worn to a Russian funeral service outside in temperatures of minus ten degrees. Three friends had come to pick me up to take me to the funeral (because my Russian would not have been good enough to take the right train to get there myself). They looked at my brown old man's jacket with curiosity and pity. 'Do you have any make-up?' one of them asked, suddenly. 'Bring it with you.' He mumbled something about 'the girls', but I didn't understand. It was very early in the morning, two of them were crying and I did not want to ask questions. I shoved a make-up bag into my handbag.

The trip there was the longest journey I had made inside Russia at that point. It took hours. We went to the end of the metro line and then on the *electrichka* (cross-country rail service). I had no idea where we were: north, south, east, west. On the way there, I remember being shocked that the boys — my friends — were smoking on the metro. I gestured and frowned at them. This was the kind of thing that could get you arrested or, at the very least, hassled, delayed or detained, which didn't seem a good idea on the way to a funeral. But they all just shrugged and looked at me reprovingly, as if to say, 'We are going to the funeral of our friend who has committed suicide. No one is going to mind us smoking on the metro in this instance.' I, however, did not smoke on the metro. I sat in accusing silence, staring at the sign on the doors that read *Ne preslonyat'sya*, which means 'Do not lean against the glass' but looks to all students of Russian as if it means 'Do not do elephant impressions.' (The word *slon* (think 'Ceylon') means 'elephant', and so it comes across as a verb that means 'to elephant around', which is maybe what leaning is, really, only using your arm instead of a trunk. This is the kind of thing that was going through my mind while I tried not to think about what had happened to Masha.)

The landscape when we arrived was straight out of *Doctor Zhivago*: fields and nothing else for miles, with a graveyard in the foreground and a few crumbling, factory-style buildings. Looking back, if I had known what was going to happen that day, I probably wouldn't have gone. The whole day involved me arranging my face into a series of expressions that indicated falsely that I wasn't shocked when, in fact, I was shocked out of my mind. We queued outside the building for a while, me not knowing why we were there or even knowing what the building was, until I realized someone was saying the word *morg* (the same word as in English). I shivered. While we were in the queue, some girls came up to me. I didn't know them. They were clearly friends of Masha's, different from the group I knew. Their faces were heavily made-up. One said, 'Are you the Foreigner? Vipulya? Tiny Little VIP?'

'Yes. I am Vipulya. I am Tiny Little VIP.'

'Did you bring the make-up?'

'Yes.'

'Can we borrow it?'

'Er, okay.'

I handed it over. A pause. The blonde girl looked at the ground. 'It's for Masha.'

Finally, I understood. They were going to make up her face with it. It was the final honour that she would be made up with Western cosmetics. Now I understood why everyone had wanted me there. That was a Clinique compact I was not going to be using again.

After about an hour standing outside in the sort of punishing cold that freezes your nostril hairs, we were ushered into the morgue, which was not much warmer in terms of temperature and positively icy in terms of immediate psychological impact. To my horror (which I was careful not to register on my face – everyone else was behaving as if this place was normal), there were corpses laid out everywhere, on slabs or slumped on chairs, maybe between fifteen and twenty, mostly older men who looked, from their unkempt appearance, as if they had died lonely and horrible homeless alcoholic deaths. One man's features were twisted into a terrible grimace.

It was something of a relief to find that Masha was laid out looking like Masha, her face peaceful and serene and glowing with recently applied Clinique blusher. I tried not to look appalled that she was wearing a white lace wedding dress.

'Nevesta Khrista' – 'a bride of Christ' – one of the girls whispered to me. We were expected to lean over and kiss her. I only pretended to do this. By this point, I had realized that I was well out of my depth and just the fact of my presence in this country where I didn't belong, among this group of friends where I didn't belong, had tipped into the horrifically inappropriate.

The next few hours are a blur. But the worst bits stick out. Having to walk for ages to the site of the grave because suicides are not allowed to be buried in the main graveyard. Her mother almost throwing herself into the grave with grief, screaming, 'My little kitten!', all the other women crying and keening. Wishing that I didn't know enough Russian to know that she was screaming, 'My little kitten!' The wake, at a horrible beige hotel where it became obvious that we were going to go round the table and say something moving about Masha and I had no idea how to say something respectful and honest in decent enough Russian. Realizing that I was going to have to eat *koliva*, which is a funeral dish of rice and sultanas and truly horrible. It's a staple of the Orthodox Church. Everyone else seemed to cheer up at the sight of the *koliva*. 'Maybe they don't get many sultanas in their diet,' I thought. It would later turn out that I was right about this.

It was one of the most upsetting and tragic days for everyone there, and I blocked it out almost as soon as it happened. In the years to come, I was to have many joyous and life-affirming experiences in Russia and with Russians. So it's unfair to let this day stand in for 'the Russian experience'. What happened was a terrible tragedy, and it was an extraordinary privilege, in a way, to witness something like this as an outsider. But it was also incredibly weird and distressing. And it did feel like fate. Whenever I questioned how Russian I could ever really be, no matter how well I learned to speak Russian, no matter how many books I read, no matter how much I tried to understand

and empathize, everything would always come back to that day and how alien I felt. I could pretend all I liked. But I would never, ever be Russian. And I would never, ever take make-up I wanted to use again to a morgue.

Of all the novels that explore Russianness in the twentieth century, *Doctor Zhivago* has marked itself out as the ultimate. The words 'fate' and 'soul' come up constantly in the novel. Death is never far off. But, this being an epic novel, it's also full of life: *Doctor Zhivago* is infused with the dirty, smoky smell of fried chicken, the stench of everyday life is barely masked by eau de cologne, and there are splashes of colour everywhere, especially mauve. (Coincidentally, also a colour Nabokov uses frequently.) Doctor Zhivago himself is in some ways the ultimate Russian literary hero: a poet and a doctor who is not quite a product of the revolution but not quite an enemy of it either. The boy we see at his mother's funeral grows up to write poems, which are reproduced at the back of the novel. Pasternak was better known as a poet before he became famous for this novel.

Doctor Zhivago was published in 1957 and swiftly translated into English. Within two years, it was at the top of the bestseller lists in the United States. In 1958, Pasternak won the Nobel Prize in Literature. The story of the novel takes place between the revolution of 1905 and the civil war, with the epilogue leading up to the 1940s. It's an intimate portrait of the damage caused by political upheaval. Zhivago the boy comes from a wealthy background. His mother has consumption and travels regularly to France and Italy to try to get better. He knows that his family name is so important it has lent itself to banks and factories. There is even such a thing as 'a Zhivago tie-pin' and a cake shaped like a rum baba known as 'a Zhivago bun'. But Zhivago's father, whom he never knew, gambled it all away and his mother and he were left poor.

The father kills himself by jumping out of a moving train. (I know. Again with the train and the suicide. Let's not even get started on this.) His lawyer, Komarovsky, travelling with him, makes everyone on the train wait while a statement is drawn up. Yuri is taken in by family friends, the Gromekos in Moscow. Their daughter Tonya is like a sister to Yuri, and an understanding arises that they will marry each other. Meanwhile, also in Moscow, an exceptionally beautiful young woman, Lara, helps her widowed mother ('a Russianized Frenchwoman') to run a struggling dressmaking business. Komarovsky acts as their patron.

When Lara turns sixteen, Komarovsky invites Lara to a ball and draws her into a sort of coercive affair. Lara's friend Pasha Antipov is distraught that she won't marry him and throws himself into revolutionary activities. Eventually Lara does marry him (Antipov) and has a child. Around the same time, Tonya and Zhivago marry. Then comes the revolution and war, many lose their homes and Moscow is evacuated. Zhivago and Lara meet properly for the first time when he is volunteering near the front line as a doctor and she as a nurse. Nothing happens between them, but he comes to associate her with the smell of an iron burning through fabric. (I know, I know. This is an extremely eventful novel. I'm summarizing it as best I can.)

Later, as the revolution takes hold, the Zhivago family escapes to the family's dacha at Yuryatin, where they think they will be safe. As 'former people' (of the middle class or aristocrats, rather than workers), they are not really safe anywhere, and Doctor Zhivago is likely to be called upon by the regime for his medical skills, something he is not happy about. By a monumental coincidence, Lara is nearby. She and Zhivago begin an affair. One day, when Tonya is heavily pregnant, Zhivago goes into town and is kidnapped by the revolutionary forces, who forcibly recruit him as their doctor. He has no way to get a message to Tonya or to Lara. Months later, he returns. Tonya has gone. Lara is still there. The two of them decamp to the Gromekos' dacha, aware that Zhivago is wanted by the authorities for his anti-regime poetry. Komarovsky, Lara's estranged suitor, comes to warn them that they are going to be arrested. Zhivago decides to let Lara and her daughter be saved. He stays and is arrested. They never see each other again.

So much fate and so much coincidence. Fate is one of the most obvious themes: '"And why is it," thought Lara, "that my fate is to see everything and take it all so much to heart?"' Personal fate is important. Especially who comes into your life at what particular moment. But historical fate is equally important: it can influence your personal fate in a positive way or totally mess everything up for you. Perhaps what Pasternak is searching for here is an answer to the question: 'How can you be yourself when you are being blown in a million different directions you can't control?'

When it was first published, the book was seen as a defence of the individual broken by the state. It's still not clear how controversial Pasternak initially intended the book to be. He said: 'The revolution is not shown at all as the cake with cream on top which it has always been made out to be as a matter of course.' That's a long way off from saying that the revolution was a waste of time. Possibly, he wanted to write a book that would be critical but would still be published and read. Or possibly, like Doctor Zhivago, he had an ambivalence about the regime: he could see the point of view of the workers, but he could also see that it had all gone horribly wrong.

Most readers of this novel have taken the view that Pasternak wanted to show a Soviet-era hero who is caught up in the sweep of events, powerless in the face of fate. That said, what little moral power Zhivago does have (to refuse to have an affair with Lara, for example), he does not exercise. He's weak and, sometimes, incredibly silly. Is that his fault, though? Or is it fate that makes him that way? Is it because of his artistic temperament? This is the traditional Russian excuse. Just think of Omar Sharif's mournful eyes and droopy, poetic moustache as Zhivago in the legendary film, and you can see the fate and the soul oozing out of him. It's that shrugging ideal: 'Woe is me. This is my fate and it's hurting my soul. I cannot help but be a weak man who abandons his pregnant wife by accident.'

I have a theory about the Russian prevalence of talk about fate and the soul. It's a way of keeping death in the conversation without actually saying, 'Oh, who cares, we're all going to die soon anyway.' But let's face it, if you are always going on about fate and the soul, then, really, you are pretty fixated on death. Long before I learned Russian or had read any Russian literature, one of the first things I knew about Russian literature was that it was about death. I had seen the film of *Doctor Zhivago*. I knew that one of Yuri Zhivago's first memories is his mother's funeral. I knew even without having read *Anna Karenina* that she throws herself under a train. Even a passing acquaintance with Russian literature leads you to the conclusion that these are not exactly books to give you inspiration for life, they're to remind you that death is never far away.

This is not to say that the experience of reading *Doctor Zhivago* is a depressing one. The opposite, actually. Because Pasternak is so upfront about death from the beginning, you accept that it is just part of life. Plus, Pasternak's style is relaxed, fluid and easygoing. He was seen as having sent the Russian novel in a completely different direction by using language that was very different to anything that had come before. The style is quite meandering and broad, and passages of the novel can appear to be a bit random. Although the plot is linear, his ideas don't have a linear development, and there are times when you are reading it almost as a history book or a series of short stories and you forget that it's a novel. Some people hate this. I rather love it.

In biographical accounts, Pasternak comes across as a serious, thoughtful, romantic man, nowhere near as tormented by spiritual crisis as Tolstoy. (It's also adorable that his name – Pasternak – means 'parsnip'. I just don't feel any British writer could have won a Nobel Prize while being called Mr Parsnip.) But he, too, had his weaknesses. For the last fourteen years of his life, his lover and secretary was Olga Ivinskaya, a woman he met in the offices of the literary magazine *Novy Mir*, where she was in charge of new authors. She was the model for Lara. Pasternak loved her but refused to leave his wife. Ivinskaya wrote an account of their time together, *A Captive of Time: My Years with Pasternak*. It's a wonderful read about that era, both nostalgic and disturbing. A lot of it, though, is a big moan about the fact that Pasternak didn't allow her, the mistress, to have her own copies of the typescript of *Doctor Zhivago*. ('Of course you expect me to get them ready and bring them to you, but there's no copy for poor me!' she writes.)

Appropriately enough for someone in love with the man who wrote one of the most haunting novels about fate ever written, Ivinskaya regards it as her fate to be bound to Pasternak. She treats her role as caretaker of his legacy as something sacred. She is also a great eyewitness to his life as a writer. One thing Ivinskaya does very well is to give colourful accounts of other people encountering *Doctor Zhivago* for the first time. I love her retelling of a meeting with the legendarily intimidating poet Anna Akhmatova. Summoned to hear Boris Pasternak read aloud from *Doctor Zhivago*, you can imagine Akhmatova listening with her eyes closed, her imperious nose twitching, one eyebrow sceptically raised. It's not clear how long this reading would have gone on for. Ivinskaya makes it sound as if he read the whole novel aloud in one sitting. (Surely that's not possible? It would take hours.) In Ivinskaya's account, Akhmatova sits regally, huddled in her 'trademark white shawl'. When Pasternak finishes reading, having greatly admired what sounds like a rather melodramatic and tremulous performance ('the inspired look on his face, the convulsive movements of his throat, and the suppressed tears in his voice'), Akhmatova pronounces. And she's not entirely complimentary. She praises the prose style ('superb') and gives the best feedback any poet can ever give by saying that it is 'as concise as poetry'.

However, she finds one major flaw. Why does Zhivago have to be ordinary? she asks. Akhmatova has a big thing about 'ordinariness' in literature. She does not like it. It's usually something she mentions in the context of Chekhov rather than Pasternak. There is something very odd about Chekhov's work, in that everything that happens in his plays and stories takes place in pre-revolutionary Russia. And yet he is someone who never mentions politics or ideology and seems almost to pretend that it's not happening. There's a certain 'whitewashed' *Downton Abbey* quality to his portrayal of pre-revolutionary Russia, the idea of sweeping all the uncomfortable social and political truths underneath the beautiful tapestry rug. Yes, in Chekhov, the characters are often miserable. But they are miserable for ordinary reasons (they're sick of looking out at birch trees, they find their sisters' company intolerable, they love people who don't love them). They are not miserable because of extraordinary historical circumstances or because they have lost their job or don't have anything to eat.

With all this in mind, Akhmatova 'could not agree with BL's [Pasternak's] own view of Zhivago as an "average" man'. It's too much like Chekhov for her. She doesn't want Pasternak's protagonist to accept the political reality, she wants him to challenge it. Akhmatova wants Zhivago to be a hero and to put himself at the centre of things. She doesn't want him to be swayed by events and unable to participate in them or change things for the better. 'She advised BL [Pasternak] to think carefully before making Zhivago a plaything of historical events instead of into a personage who tried to influence them in some way.' She almost alludes to the fact that Pasternak has chickened out. He is supposed to be a poet even before he is a novelist, and yet he hasn't found what she calls 'a poetic solution'. He hasn't found a way to make Zhivago part of the action, calling the shots, not just swayed by fate.

This is a fascinating criticism of *Doctor Zhivago*. One of the things that has always irritated me – and many readers and critics – about the novel is that everything that happens is all very convenient for the good doctor. For a novel about fate, perhaps it's not surprising that its chief flaw is the role of coincidence. The amount of coincidence is almost comical. Your mother's died? Here's a lovely new family for you. Lonely and in need of a wife? Why not marry the adopted sister and best friend (Tonya) you've been brought up with your whole life! Slightly bored in your marriage and lonely while serving as a doctor at the front? Why, here's a lovely nurse (Lara) who has crossed your path several times before. Frustrated and inflamed by passion miles away from anywhere in the Urals? Don't worry, Lara's here, too! Annoyed your affair with Lara is due to be cut short as your wife is pregnant with a second child? Fear not! You can get kidnapped so that your family thinks you've disappeared and, when you come back, you can live in your deserted family house with Lara as your mistress! Hurrah! Whenever fate intervenes in Zhivago's life, it really does make things very convenient for him indeed. But aren't we all like this, really? If a convenient solution presents itself, we accept it. We grab hold of coincidences as a way out, and to avoid having to make decisions and change direction in life ourselves. Pasternak doesn't judge us for this. He sees it as human. How do you face life? You roll with it, even if it makes you look bad. It's as if he's asking: 'What's the difference between fate and convenience?' Not much. And most of us follow the path of least resistance. It's only when we look back that we think to ourselves: 'Ah, yes, that must have been meant to be. It was fate!' Actually, it happened that way because we are morally weak and lazy. Not that Pasternak is judgemental about this. He just tells it like it is.

The big question in *Doctor Zhivago* is whether this level of coincidence is entirely normal and true to life. And it really is an extraordinary level of coincidence. (The fact that Komarovsky is both a) Zhivago's father's lawyer from the train incident at the beginning of the book and b) connected to the woman Zhivago falls in love with is fairly far-fetched. There must have been thousands of lawyers in Moscow at the time. What were the odds?) But it strikes me that there's something about Russia itself that forces a Russian novel to contain ridiculous amounts of coincidence. (There are also many such extreme unlikelihoods in *War and Peace*.) If you are Tolstoy or Pasternak and you want to cover the scope and sweep of Russia in your novel, you are going to have to cover vast distances geographically in order to represent the whole of Russia, seeing as Russia is the world's largest country by land mass. Whether they're conscious or not of this fact (and there is a theory that we can't help but be very different kinds of people, according to the size and geography of the country we call our own), it pervades their work. And so, in *War and Peace*, when Andrei is convalescing miles away from home, who should be the one person who is nearby, even though he is in the middle of nowhere? Why, of course, it is Natasha.

In *Doctor Zhivago*, the other ridiculous but necessary unlikelihood is that Lara goes to Yuryatin, which is a town very near where the family of Zhivago's wife, Tonya, owns property. Yuryatin is over seven hundred miles from Moscow. Of all the places Lara could go . . . Of course, it would not make for a very good novel if Zhivago thought: 'Well, it's just happenstance that Lara is here. I must ignore her for the sake of my marriage. To go off with her on the strength of a geographical coincidence . . . Well, that would be weak and immoral.'

This novel asks us what we think of the moral condition of the person who gives in to the power of fate. Usually, in Russian literature, these types are seen as human and understandable. Yuri and Lara's relationship is represented as the greatest love story ever told. It is not represented as a man taking advantage of a preposterous coincidence to cheat on his wife. No. Lara is there because they are destined to be together. Man is powerless in the face of destiny. And destiny is to be respected because it lets us off the hook. We spend our whole lives looking for things that are meant to be, hoping that fate will guide us, rather than taking responsibility for our own choices.

And yet. The novel shows that fate does not make us happy and give us what we want. Sometimes it brings a much-loved mistress seven hundred miles from Moscow and into the back of beyond, where we just happen to be. But at other times it is just as likely to be cruel. At the end of *Doctor Zhivago*, Yuri returns to Moscow to live with a third woman. (I know! Don't get me started.) Tonya has gone to Paris. Lara has disappeared with Komarovsky. Zhivago's life becomes difficult. He is unhappy and not physically well. He eventually dies of a heart attack.

In the film, there is one more insane coincidence: Zhivago is back in Moscow, travelling by tram. He sees Lara in the street. (This doesn't happen in the book.) He tries to get the tram to stop to get to her, but he can't. His distress mounts, and he stumbles off the train to die in the street, while she walks past him, oblivious. In the book, the ending is even more symbolic. As he is about to go into cardiac arrest, Zhivago glimpses a woman from the tram. It's Madame Fleury, the old woman who used to work in the place where he first realized he loved Lara (when she burned the ironing). Madame Fleury is wearing a mauve dress. Mauve was the colour of a dress Lara once wore. It's also the colour Pasternak uses to describe Russia before the revolution: it represents innocence, purity, idealism. It's the colour he glimpses before he dies. 'He thought of several people whose lives run parallel and close together but at different speeds, and wondered in what circumstances some of them would overtake and survive others.'

The odds of something like this happening in real life are zero. But, then, real life is actually more ridiculous and full of coincidences than novels, which is why a novel like *Doctor Zhivago* can get away with what is really a ridiculous plot and go on to be one of the best-loved novels of all time. Our lives do run parallel and close together with the lives of others, and so often we do feel powerless in the face of fate. What did it mean that I knew a woman who killed herself as soon as I moved to Russia? Why did she die then, and I am still alive now? The answer to these questions in *Doctor Zhivago* is brutal. It's coincidence. It's fate. It's dumb luck. How do you cope with that in life? You just keep going, even if it means sometimes being an inadequate person, betraying people you love or running away from responsibility. You just keep going.

3. How to be Optimistic in the Face of Despair: *Requiem* by Anna Akhmatova

(Or: Don't wear tight shoes on prison visits)

For someone a fresh breeze blows
For someone the sunset luxuriates —
We wouldn't know, we are those who everywhere
Hear only the rasp of the hateful key

I first discovered Anna Akhmatova's poetry when I was living in St Petersburg during the year that had started with Masha's funeral. It was a happy year, for the most part. But there were many times when I was confronted by the realities of the lives of Russian friends and had to dig deep to find any sense of optimism. Generally speaking, the people around me had very little money and not always that much food. If they had work, it was precarious. If you opened someone's fridge, it would be virtually bare. It was very common for friends to ask me to lend them five dollars to last them to the end of the month. (They would almost always return it.) You had to be careful about helping people, though. First, you couldn't help everyone. And, second, you can't be friends or equals with people if you're their benefactor. Overall, life could be wearing. I frequently felt guilty and helpless. At the end of that year, when I returned home to England to my parents' house, without thinking, I went to get some milk to make tea. When I opened the fridge, I was so shocked at the sight of the packed shelves that I burst into tears.

The one thing that always made me feel better was reading

Anna Akhmatova. She's not an obvious candidate to choose as someone to cheer you up. Few writers have catalogued misery in such forensic, lyrical detail:

> In the terrible years of the Yezhov terror I spent seventeen months waiting in line outside the prison in Leningrad. One day somebody in the crowd identified me. Standing behind me was a woman, with lips blue from the cold, who had, of course, never heard me called by name before. Now she started out of the torpor common to us all and asked me in a whisper (everyone whispered there): 'Can you describe this?' And I said: 'I can.' Then something like a smile passed fleetingly over what had once been her face.
>
> – 1 April 1957, Leningrad

This is the opener to Akhmatova's cycle of poems *Requiem*, about the experience of women waiting for news of relatives who were arrested in the 1930s. Composed between 1935 and 1940, at a time when the population of the prison camps almost doubled, *Requiem* was not published until 1962, in Munich, and even then without the knowledge or consent of the author. It is an eleven-page poem about the worst imaginings of people pining for their loved ones and about not knowing whose fate is worse, the ones sent away or the ones left behind:

> Mountains bow down to this grief,
> Mighty rivers cease to flow.
> . . .
> For someone a fresh breeze blows
> For someone the sunset luxuriates –
> We wouldn't know, we are those who everywhere
> Hear only the rasp of the hateful key
>
> . . .

And it's not clear to me
Who is a beast now, who is a man
And how long before the execution.

We are not talking Doris Day here. And yet, somehow, Akhmatova always finds a chink of light:

But hope keeps singing from afar
. . .
Never mind, I was ready. I will manage somehow.

Today I have so much to do;
I must kill memory once and for all,
I must turn my soul to stone,
I must learn to live again –

Akhmatova has a sense of the theatrical, and she makes everything into a game, distracting herself – and us – from the worst of life, by playing with words. In the introduction to *Requiem*, she quotes a woman in the prison queue who asks her: 'Can you describe this?' The word for 'describe' in Russian – *opisat'* – contains the root of the word 'to write' – *pisat'*. It's not just a rhetorical question about whether she can find the words to describe this situation. The woman is actively asking Akhmatova to write about it. In a very simple way, she is saying, 'Someone needs to bear witness. You're a writer. Do you think you're up to it?' Akhmatova tells the horror of an everyday moment very simply and without melodrama. She is the voice of a time when no one wanted to speak. If you want a dose of grit just when you think that everything is hopeless and you are about to give up, Akhmatova always has something elegant and inspiring to say. In *Requiem*, she says it best:

Forget how that detested door slammed shut
And an old woman howled like a wounded animal
And may the melting snow stream like tears
From my motionless lids of bronze,
And a prison dove coo in the distance,
And the ships of the Neva sail calmly on.

Sadly, though, beyond Russia, Akhmatova's name is now barely known to anyone outside academic circles or those who take a special interest in Russian literature or poetry. This is a horrific development, as Akhmatova's status within her lifetime was huge. Born in 1889, she was a sort of Russian Virginia Woolf. Later on, she became the unofficial dissident poet for the Stalinist age, writing her secret poetry about the horrors of waiting in line for news from the Gulag. I don't think there is an English-language poet whose appeal comes close to that she has for Russians, and their love of her is compounded by the fact that she is easily the most famous female figure in Russian literature, full stop. Professionally persecuted, psychologically tortured and ostracized by the state, she made it to the age of seventy-six, outliving not only many of her peers but also Stalin himself. She never stopped writing. She never stopped trying to make a difference. And, perhaps most extraordinary of all, she never stopped hoping. She may possibly be one of the most optimistic people ever to have lived.

In St Petersburg in the 1990s, it was assumed that you were interested in Akhmatova if you were a) learning Russian and b) a woman. You couldn't possibly be serious about learning Russian if you hadn't read any of Akhmatova's poetry, especially if you were a woman. And you would – of course! – have a special understanding of it if you were a woman. I was slightly sceptical of this way of thinking, especially as her poetry seemed to me to be about knuckling down and facing life's biggest challenges. I always felt a bit uncomfortable about the whole Akhmatova/ woman thing. The poetry of her contemporary and close friend Osip Mandelstam, for example, is similar in tone and subject matter to Akhmatova's and just as enticing. There can be an uncomfortable sexism in the fawning appreciation of Akhmatova. But we will set that aside, because any road to her is a good road, even if she is such a steely and formidable character that her work can initially seem intimidating.

Akhmatova's gender weighed heavily on her during her lifetime: she knew that everything she wrote would be assumed to represent 'the woman's experience'. And yet, at the same time, her work was criticized for being 'too much about the woman's experience'. No wonder she had to be ballsy and determined just to keep going. Her writing is harsh and clear-eyed:

> No, not under the vault of alien skies
> And not under the shelter of alien wings –
> I was with my people, then,
> There, where my people, unfortunately, were.

Is there any better way of saying: 'This really happened to us. I was there. And it was hell.'

As if all this wasn't already a huge burden, much of her work was produced in impossible circumstances. She couldn't have it published because she was not on the list of writers approved by the state. She couldn't even physically write anything down because her home was routinely searched by the KGB, as were the homes of all her friends. It was illegal not only to publish anti-state material, but to write it in the first place. To prevent them being confiscated, Akhmatova's poems were preserved in what was known as 'pre-Gutenberg conditions'. They were part of oral history, not written down, just remembered, in the way poetry was 'written' (i.e. committed to memory) for years before print was invented. Nadezhda Mandelstam, the wife of the poet Osip, writes about how impressed she was with Akhmatova's discretion as she worked on her poetry. Nadezhda had witnessed her own husband speaking the verses to himself and judged that Akhmatova was much less overt. 'She did not even allow her lips to move, as M. did so openly, but rather, I think, pressed them tighter as she composed her poems, and her mouth became set in an even sadder way.'

In the early 1960s Akhmatova revealed that she had entrusted a handful of people with her work: 'Eleven people knew *Requiem* by heart, and not one of them betrayed me,' she said. Some poems were not written down anywhere until years later. Fortunately, Akhmatova's friend Lydia Chukovskaya had an extraordinary gift for memorizing poetry. She and Akhmatova had a method: 'Suddenly in mid-conversation, she would fall silent and, signalling to me with her eyes at the ceiling and walls, she would get a scrap of paper and a pencil.' Akhmatova would then say something for the censors (who had bugged the apartment) to hear. Two popular choices were: 'Would you like some tea?' Or 'You're very tanned.' Then she would note down a couple of lines on the scrap of paper and hand it to Chukovskaya to memorize. (I don't even want to think about the pressure that this poor reader was under.) Once Chukovskaya had learned her lines, she would hand the piece of paper back and Akhmatova would say loudly, 'How early autumn came this year.' She would then burn the scraps of paper over an ashtray. I can't begin to imagine the presence of mind Akhmatova must have had to keep it together mentally under these conditions. She clearly put 'dignified survival' at the top of her list and refused to compromise in any way.

And yet. Akhmatova can still be regarded as inconsequential or unimportant because she is a woman. (Whenever I think about this, I want to summon Tolstoy from beyond the grave to throw eggs at her detractors. He would do it because, as we have established, he would do practically anything as long as it involved eggs.) This is even more insulting when you consider the subtext of *Requiem*, her greatest work: it is a written record of the thoughts and feelings of the women who suffered the consequences of the Stalinist purges, waiting outside the prisons for news:

> I see you, I hear you, I feel you:
>
> The one they almost had to drag at the end,
> And the one who tramps her native land no more,
> And the one who, tossing her beautiful head,
> Said, 'Coming here's like coming home.'
> . . .
> And if they gag my exhausted mouth
> Through which a hundred million scream,
> Then may the people remember me
> On the eve of my remembrance day.

To reduce Akhmatova's work to 'women's poetry for women' (which is often what happens) is to miss the point entirely: she wrote this to make sure this experience was never forgotten.

But in Russia, even as recently as the mid-1990s, people remained accustomed to a sort of deference towards women that verged on something out of Jane Austen's time, as I discovered when I lived there. It was common for men to kiss you on the hand upon meeting you, to pull your chair out for you, light your cigarette, pour your wine. There's a 1997 documentary made in St Petersburg about a group of people all turning forty on the same day, and at one of the birthday parties a man says humbly to his lady friend, almost lisping with obsequiousness: 'Please, may I cut you a thinner gherkin?' If people were drinking, the first toast would be to the person hosting the party. The second would be 'to the lovely ladies'. At parties, there was a general assumption that 'the ladies love sweet things', and people made a great show of bringing out cakes and chocolates at every social event 'for the ladies'. Because ladies must have a sweet tooth! And ladies must love poetry written by another lady! This was the context in which people read Akhmatova during the Soviet era, and in the period immediately afterwards.

This is all nonsense, of course. Akhmatova has bigger balls than Hunter S. Thompson, Norman Mailer and Ernest Hemingway combined. When I think of her playing the KGB at their own game, carefully recruiting the right circle of trusted people to learn her poems by heart and scribbling things on paper only to set light to them minutes later, all to avoid being killed for writing poetry . . . Well, it makes me want to scream. Or wield a samurai sword. The highest expression of femininity? I don't think so. This is the bravest of human acts. It has nothing to do with being a lady. It's about being someone who 'stood for three hundred hours/And where they never unbolted the doors for me'.

Those who appreciate Akhmatova know that to understand her is to understand – deeply – what it was to survive the Soviet era. *Requiem* itself is beautiful and intense. And, although I would always be wary of disparaging work in translation of any kind, it has to be said that Akhmatova's poetry works particularly well in translation, compared to a lot of Russian poetry. It can be read without you remotely feeling that it was written in another language. The themes of the pre-revolution poetry are love, passion, sex, betrayal. After the revolution, Akhmatova has little choice but to write about Russia's past and future, the difficulties of the everyday Soviet experience and the thing she's best known for: her testimony about life outside the prison gates, waiting for news of relatives. Akhmatova uses clear, sharp images, flashes of sound, light and feeling, biblical references mixed in with snippets of dialogue. If you read her in English, you don't necessarily get the rhythm and the rhyme, but you can get a vivid picture and a measure of her impact. I will happily read any of her poetry in English. It's different to the original but no less beautiful.

Akhmatova's reputation as the glamorous face of women's literature is tricky, though. It's wrong, in a way, to mythologize Akhmatova, as she really did have the most awful life. Her first husband was killed by the secret police. Her son and common-law husband both spent many years in the Gulag. She was never arrested or imprisoned herself, but she lived with the burden of having caused suffering to those closest to her. She was also under constant surveillance. Stalin took a particular interest in her.

Despite all this, it would be unfair not to point out that she was ridiculously, impossibly, chic. She even resembled Virginia Woolf physically (down to the same nose), and she dressed like a member of the Bloomsbury set, even if her clothes were threadbare and worn. She had an aristocratic bearing. It became her mission to capture the unspoken, subconscious schism in Soviet life. Akhmatova became the mouthpiece for what she called 'the two Russias' that were staring each other in the eye: 'the ones in the camps and the ones who had put them there'. This was something she said to her friend Lydia Chukovskaya. It's a perfect description of the Soviet system. She wrote poems that reflected the dualities of Russia's story over the last hundred years: people who support the system and people who inwardly resist it; people who want things to change and people who fear change; the public face versus the private face.

Even before this era of horror, Akhmatova had not had an easy life. Her earlier poetry, which had made her famous, marked her out as bourgeois, pro-Tsarist, Western, a traitor. And yet she had no desire to leave Russia. She was rejected from the accepted list of Soviet writers, which meant she had no hope of any kind of income. She became a sort of non-person. For a long time, she had no idea what to write about, and the poems did not come. 'My name was struck off the list of the living . . . And after accepting the experience of those years – terror, weariness, emptiness, deathly isolation – in 1936 I began to write again, but my handwriting had changed, my voice sounded different.' It was during this time that *Requiem* surfaced, a collection which bridged the gap between the romantic poet she had always been and the political poet she was forced to become by circumstance. 'There could be no return to my earlier manner. Which is better, which worse . . . It's not for me to say.' She hated that *Requiem*, when it eventually came out, was criticized in the West for being an example of her being past her best, having had too big a gap in her writing. They didn't understand anything about how difficult it had been for her to go on at all.

She was also forced to become a more practical person than she probably ever wanted to be. She certainly adopted a 'diva' stance when she didn't want to deal with people. But the reality of Soviet life obliged her to engage with the mundane. When she hears the news that her son, Lev, is being sent to the camps in the north in 1939, she does a whip-round to find warm clothes: '. . . getting a hat from one person, a scarf from another, gloves from another'. (There is nothing to buy in the shops, even if she has the money.) The next day, she has to wait so long in line at the prison to hand over the parcel that her feet swell up and she can barely walk. One account has her taking her shoes off to walk barefoot across the prison courtyard. After this visit she wrote 'To Death', the eighth poem of *Requiem*, where she asks death to come for her: 'You will come in any case – so why not now?'

Despite the gloomy themes of Akhmatova's work and the appalling personal tragedy she was living through, somehow she found some kind of weak but sustainable optimism. It's a quiet inner self-belief that nurtures your integrity and says: 'The external circumstances are what they are. Deep inside me, there is a part of me that will never be crushed.' This was reflected in her elegance and her glamour, which she exuded both in her appearance and in her work. Optimism requires some kind of control. To take control over your thoughts is the start of optimism. Just the other day, I was telling a friend who was feeling upset about not being in a relationship that digging deep to find optimism would be a good move. I'm sure she wanted to hit me. But, unfortunately, it's true: when we are at our lowest and feel that we have no control, we need to find advantages in our situation, however creative we need to be to do so. It gives us back control.

Akhmatova survived by being alluring, courageous and haughty. She also had an attractive wit about her. Perhaps the person with whom Akhmatova had the most jocular relationship was her friend Mandelstam. He had known her for many years. As Mandelstam's widow, Nadezhda, writes in her wonderful memoir, *Hope against Hope*, Akhmatova used to come and stay with them in their apartment and, in her honour, they would cover their stove with a tarpaulin to serve as a tablecloth so that it looked like they had done something special for their guest. One time Akhmatova came to visit, Mandelstam went out to scrounge food from neighbours for some supper for her. He came back with one egg. Later, after the secret police had been round to search the apartment for manuscripts, the lone egg was still sitting on the makeshift table. (Good job Tolstoy was not around.) 'You eat it,' Akhmatova told Mandelstam, drily. On another occasion, he met her at the station. Her train was very late and he said to her, teasing, 'You travel at the same speed as Anna Karenina.' As if she had taken so long to arrive that she had come from the nineteenth century.

Akhmatova was 'allowed' to live while others around her were rounded up and sent to the camps or to their execution from the early 1930s onwards. Mandelstam had written an extremely risky poem directly referencing Stalin. It was later referred to as a 'sixteen-line death sentence'. Akhmatova would have heard this poem. It was as if Mandelstam was tempting fate, having said, 'Poetry is respected only in this country – people are killed for it. There's no place where more people are killed for it.' To be fair, a writer could be killed for their work whether they had written something directly referencing Stalin or not. It was arbitrary and unpredictable. But when Mandelstam read the incriminating lines to Pasternak, the author of *Doctor Zhivago* said: 'What you just read . . . is not poetry, it is suicide. You didn't read it to me, I didn't hear it, and I beg you not to read this to anyone.' It was this poem that was supposed to have played a role in the arrests of Mandelstam, Akhmatova's common-law husband Punin and her son, Lev Gumilev – and led indirectly to the experiences which Akhmatova wrote about in *Requiem*. Mandelstam was initially put under the order of 'isolate but preserve'. He died in a transit camp near Vladivostok, not long afterwards.

The pressure he was under during this time must have been unbearable. Akhmatova had a temper on her and did not suffer fools gladly. Nadezhda writes of the time when the secret police were constantly coming for people: 'This was why we had outlawed the question, "What was he arrested for?" "What for?" Akhmatova would cry indignantly whenever, infected by the prevailing climate, anyone of our circle asked this question. "What do you mean, what for? It's time you understood that people are arrested for nothing!"'

Even setting aside the psychological impact of the punishment dealt out to others related to her (who were essentially arrested in her place), it's hard to imagine how Akhmatova kept her mind together throughout all the years of surveillance.

When her KGB file was released in the 1990s, there were over nine hundred pages detailing phone-tapped and recorded conversations, denunciations and confessions from people she knew. At one point, Akhmatova lived with Nadezhda in Tashkent, and the two of them would return to their apartment to find things disturbed in some way, as if a search had taken place. Once, Nadezhda found a lipstick out on a table, next to a mirror that had been moved from another room. Brilliantly, she takes great pleasure in saying that she knew the lipstick wasn't hers or Akhmatova's because it was 'of a revoltingly loud shade'. Nadezhda herself writes so evocatively, and even humorously, of this appalling time, describing Akhmatova as having lived through an era that was 'vegetarian' before things turned nasty under Stalin.

Akhmatova, like other writers such as Bulgakov and, to some extent, Pasternak, had a relationship with Stalin of sorts, although they never had a direct encounter with him or a phone call from him. Stalin knew of her existence and made it his business to make sure she suffered. On one particularly bad occasion, she went to Bulgakov for help, knowing that he had once written a letter to Stalin which had its desired effect. (This may be the one and only instance of anyone ever writing a letter to Stalin that ended in a positive result. In general, writing letters to Stalin was at best foolish and a waste of time, and at worst, dangerous.) Bulgakov's wife, Yelena Sergeyevna, writes of that time in her diary: 'During the day there was a ring at the door. I went out and there was Akhmatova with such a dreadful face, and so much thinner, that I scarcely recognized her; nor did Misha [Bulgakov]. It turned out that in one and the same night both her husband and her son had been arrested. She had come to deliver a letter to Yosif Vissarionovich [Stalin]. She was quite clearly in a confused state and was muttering things to herself.'

What kept Akhmatova going, of course, was her work. The

circumstances in which she composed her poetry were ridiculous, unbelievable and depressing. And yet she remained proud and stylish, almost until the end. (By the end of her life, in 1966, she had put on a lot of weight and looked distinctly unwell. Who can blame her for giving up just a little bit? Any normal person would have given up years before.) I wonder if she sometimes relished the drama of it all, while hating it at the same time. According to the theatre critic Vitaly Vilenkin, even in the thick of all this Akhmatova never really lost her glamorous touch. At a reading in 1938, he writes: 'At first I imagined she was wearing something very elegant. But what I mistook for an original gown for special occasions turned out to be a black silk dressing gown with some kind of white dragon embroidered on it and very old – the silk was in places quite threadbare.' Another account mentions her wearing a black silk dressing gown split along the seam from the shoulder to the knee. In my mind's eye, Akhmatova is like Norma Desmond in *Sunset Boulevard*, always ready for her close-up, clinging on to the limelight, despite knowing deep inside that times have moved on. Back in 1915, writing about the time in her life when she had tuberculosis, she said: 'Every morning I got up, put on a silk peignoir and went to bed again.' She never quite gave up being that person, and thank God for that.

In her youth, Akhmatova had been one of the gilded youth of the pre-revolutionary era, a celebrated poet and doyenne of the nightclub scene and the Stray Dog literary café, dressed all in black and wearing a necklace of black agate. As Elaine Feinstein writes in her superb biography, Akhmatova was in her element among a clientele who 'took pleasure in chilled Chablis'. She wrote poems that celebrated and cursed her 'open marriage' with Gumilev, a fellow poet. She wrote about wearing 'my tightest skirt, to look even more svelte' at evenings at the Stray Dog, where she hung out with a crowd who were, basically, all sleeping with each other, then constantly threatening to commit suicide when, every now and again, the details blew wide open. (Several of this circle did commit suicide before 1917, in dramatic, poetic ways.)

She wrote about love, sex (often phrased as 'intimacy'), betrayal, adultery, about what it was like to be a mistress and to be cast aside as a mistress. For her, this became the stuff of great poetry. But it was also the stuff of being middle class (if not virtually of the aristocratic class), of being bohemian, intellectual and, to a greater or lesser extent at different times, moneyed. This was in direct contrast to the poetry she was to write during the Stalin era and to the degrading conditions, both financial and social, in which she then found herself. As a young woman, she might have identified at least partly as being European (she spoke French). But she later made her choice and was dubbed 'Anna of all the Russias' by fellow legendary poetess Marina Tsvetaeva.

She always comes across in everything that has been written about her as someone who would have loved to ignore politics and focus purely on the romance and tragedy of life. Her world is one of emotions. Politics forces its cold reason and logic on her. (Not that there was much logic and reason in the Soviet system. Or, if there was, it was often applied erratically and sometimes nonsensically.) It's impossible to imagine for a second that Akhmatova relished her role as a witness to a historical era. She would much rather have been writing a sonnet about tight black skirts that make you look slimmer. But the Soviet experience was about forcing people to be serious and to live with a life-and-death situation even if they were not remotely interested in politics. Ironically and stupidly, to be uninterested was of course in itself a political act.

Appropriately enough, though, I was first introduced to Akhmatova's work by one of my most feminine and sweetest Russian friends. Halfway through my student year in Russia, I got to know a nurse called Tanya. She was a quiet but self-possessed figure, not physically unlike Julie Christie as Lara in *Doctor Zhivago*. She wasn't like a lot of my other friends: she was very softly spoken, shy, not keen to drink too much (completely uncharacteristic of the group I was hanging out with) and had very little interest in my status as a foreigner. In short, she was a breath of fresh air and felt like a true friend. I very quickly took to her as someone genuine, kind and selfless. In view of her professional qualifications, our friendship was especially handy for me as, shortly after we got to know each other, I contracted dysentery. It was not as appalling a life experience as seeing everyone you love sent to the Gulag, but it was still horrible. I caught it from eating in an Indian restaurant, which was, I seem to remember, the only Indian restaurant in St Petersburg at the time. A Russian friend said solemnly, only part-joking: 'This is what happens when you eat in bourgeois restaurants.' Tanya's ability to nurse me back to health endeared her to me (she barely knew me, and no one was forcing her to do this), and she was also wonderful to listen to when talking about poetry. She was the gateway drug to Akhmatova, with whom Tanya was obsessed, with me following, puppy-like, swiftly behind.

Tanya was a good person to know if you had dysentery. She was medically qualified, had access to certain medications and came to look after me in person, insisting that I swallow packets of black powder that I later realized were something not dissimilar to ground-up coal. I did not know that charcoal is a medieval remedy for stomach complaints. Some things you have to learn by experience. Or even by repeatedly ingesting powdered coal.

She read Akhmatova poems to me and performed weird rituals over my body (clothed, I hasten to add), running her hands above me as if she could sense a presence, closing her eyes and humming, then flicking the 'evil' away. I thought it was extremely odd, but I didn't want to question her authority. I also wanted to pretend to be Russian and not be a lily-livered foreigner. (In fact, unbeknownst to me, she was turning me into a charcoal-livered foreigner.) So I made out to her and to myself that I thought all this was totally normal. I later realized what she was doing was very similar to reiki, the alternative remedy now much beloved of Hollywood types. So, Tanya was ahead of her time. After about a week of intense pain and suffering and consuming large quantities of coal which passed straight through me, I eventually got over the dysentery. But not before paying $150 cash for a visit from an American doctor who prescribed some antibiotics.

After this, I discovered that Tanya attended poetry evenings where she and others would recite Akhmatova from memory in an intense, dramatic style. It was perhaps the most Russian of all Russian things I had witnessed. Being theatrical, ambitious and increasingly imagining myself to be Russian in the depths of my soul, I decided that I, too, must become a part of this, and I asked her to coach me in the reading of an Akhmatova poem. Reading Akhmatova's poetry to yourself is like splashing your face with cold water. Learning her verses by heart and reciting them in a room of devotees is like dancing naked under a waterfall.

I would spend long afternoons at Tanya's apartment contorting my vowel sounds to perfect a recitation which was as lyrically, authentically Russian as possible. She nodded solemnly and occasionally tutted when I stumbled over a word. I suspect it was like trying to teach the policeman from the 1980s TV series *'Allo 'Allo* to read Shakespeare. (This man was English but pretending to be French, even though his French (rendered in English) was terrible: 'Good moaning. I was just pissing by your door . . .') I knew I was mangling Akhmatova's lyrical renderings of 'hard grains of swirling snow' into something that sounded like 'hart grans of swoolly snook', but we persevered. When we rehearsed at Tanya's apartment, her five-year-old son would sit playing with a toy truck in the corner. Without fail, every time I left the flat, half an hour later he would murmur to her mournfully, knowing that I was from England: 'I guess she must be flying over us right now.' He imagined that every time I visited I flew over from England in an aeroplane, then flew back again. In fact I lived about four metro stops away.

Because of its simplicity, Akhmatova's poetry is easy to commit to memory, even for an idiot foreigner like me. The only challenge was making it sound Russian enough to be read aloud without offending Akhmatova's legacy. When Tanya and I finally went to our first public recital of Akhmatova's poetry, I had practised for months, and delivered my lines in as natural a Russian way as I could possibly muster, casting aside all thoughts of French/English policemen: 'Nothing is changed; against the dining room windows, hard grains of snow still beat . . .' Tanya kissed me at the end. 'You got away with it.' We drank a toast. Not 'to the lovely ladies'. But 'to Akhmatova'. I hope she would have been proud. In many stories about her life, Akhmatova asks for vodka when everyone else is drinking wine. Lydia Chukovskaya writes: 'She always asked for vodka and always drank two or three glasses, her habitual toast being, "Let's drink a toast that we shall again sit down together and that we shall meet again."' See what I mean? That's proper optimism.

4. How to Survive Unrequited Love: *A Month in the Country* by Ivan Turgenev
(Or: Don't fall in love with your best friend's wife)

'Love of every kind, happy as much as unhappy, is a real calamity if you give yourself up to it completely.'

I found out about Turgenev's existence at a crucial moment. There had been a very small leap between me obsessing over *Anna Karenina* in my mid-teens and deciding that learning Russian was my destiny. There was, unsurprisingly, an even smaller leap between me becoming obsessed with learning Russian and me becoming obsessed with unsuitable men who spoke Russian. This culminated, during my year abroad, in my acquaintance with a man whose name – Bogdan Bogdanovich – translated as God's Gift, Son of God's Gift. In many ways, he lived up to his name.

He was a man whom I loved with the passion that Anna Karenina first felt for Vronsky, but he regarded me with as much affection as Levin held for the ladies who stank of eau de vinaigre. This is where Turgenev comes in. No one writes better about unrequited love. Real life is about quiet, slow, awkward moments of humiliation. And what greater humiliation is there than loving someone far, far more than they love you? This is the kind of embarrassing self-inflicted fever that Turgenev, arguably the most English of all the Russian writers, is brilliant at describing. In *A Month in the Country* a man falls in love with his best friend's wife. I didn't covet anyone's spouse. But I did fall in love with a man who didn't really want to belong to me.

In August 1994, I was twenty-one years old and spending the

summer by the Black Sea, Odessa, Ukraine. It was the last few months of my year abroad. That summer was a blur of strong cigarettes, black bread, tea and jam, whispered invitations on a Saturday night: 'Just one little rumochka' (a shot glass of moonshine). 'Come on – *davai* – fifty grams.' I spent a lot of time drinking *samogon* ('moonshine'), eating pig fat and being in love. He was in a rock band. He was the lead guitarist. They played songs in terrible English with titles like 'I'm Not Drunk, It's Only F***ing Funk'. I was his groupie. He was my world. We went to his gigs together. We went to other people's gigs together. We went everywhere together. We kissed. We laughed. We ate pig fat. Pig fat is a big treat in Ukraine. I had got used to eating huge slabs of it on hunks of black bread. I loved a bit of pig fat. There was only one problem in paradise. I was drunk a lot of the time, but I was never too drunk to know that God's Gift, Son of God's Gift, did not love me in the same way that I loved him.

Somewhere buried inside me was a homesickness for England and, buried deeper still, the knowledge that I was falling deeper into a situation where I was going to have to choose between two worlds. The closer it got to September, the more I didn't want to go home. The drunker I got, the more I loved him. The drunker I got, the more Russian I felt. The drunker I got, the happier I was to stay . . . and the deeper I fell in love with someone who was very much not the right person and who didn't love me back. It was that horrible feeling of wanting something you know you shouldn't want and isn't going to do you any good at all, but still wanting it anyway.

Anna Karenina was no help in solving this problem. She and Vronsky have loads of problems, but an unevenness of feeling is not really one of them. Luckily, as well as ploughing my way through Tolstoy with a dictionary at the time, I happened to be reading Turgenev's play *A Month in the Country* in translation. It is a cruelly hilarious cautionary tale about unrequited love.

Turgenev himself experienced this unhappy state for more or less the entirety of his sixty-four years. From around the 1840s to the end of his life in 1883, Turgenev adored the married opera singer Pauline Viardot. The exact nature of their relationship is hotly debated. But it would seem to me to be one of the most extreme examples of one-sided love in history. Certainly, she loved him to some extent, but he was definitely the weaker partner in the couple. Turgenev represents his complicated feelings about this state of being through the unfortunate character of Rakitin.

No character illustrates Turgenev's state of hopeless anticipation better than the mournful, resigned, comically self-pitying Rakitin. To imagine his adorable face, think of Ralph Fiennes at his most apologetic and subservient. (He played Rakitin in a 2014 Russian film version. He does the best job he possibly can, having learned Russian in three months in order to play the role. But they still had to overdub his voice with a native actor, as Russian audiences couldn't understand what he was saying.) Rakitin is described as a thirty-year-old 'friend of the family'. You have to wonder if Turgenev was making his own little joke here, as he frequently referred to himself as a 'friend of the family' when explaining his connection to Viardot. I now can't hear the expression 'friend of the family' without thinking that the person is trying secretly to intimate that they are having an affair with someone in the family. Which is awkward, as it's a fairly common expression to describe a completely innocent relationship and now, whenever I hear it, I adopt an involuntary expression that says, 'Oh, no one believes you. There is clearly something else going on here. "Friend of the family", indeed.'

Rakitin is the ultimate doomed lover, convinced that no one has ever loved anyone as much as he loves the woman who will never love him (who is, unhelpfully, although actually helpfully as regards proximity and social availability, his best friend's wife): 'It's my belief . . . that love of every kind, happy as much as unhappy, is a real calamity if you give yourself up to it completely.' He gives himself up to the calamity anyway – of course.

Written as 'a comedy in five acts', the play is set at the country dacha of the Islayev family. The husband, a wealthy landowner, Arkady, is thirty-six. His wife, Natalya Petrovna, is twenty-nine. Yes, Turgenev lists the exact ages of the protagonists. It's common to give age guidelines for characters in plays (Chekhov does it, too), but it's unusual to do it for every single one, as Turgenev does. It makes you feel like he's making a bit of a point. He wants to underline the age differences and generational rivalries.

This is already a mildly disastrous love triangle between two old friends (Islayev and Rakitin) and Islayev's wife, Natalya. Largely indifferent towards her husband, Natalya is not interested in Rakitin either, although she toys with him a little, as he's better company than the man she is married to. There can't just be one pocket of misery, though. With two men already pining for a woman who doesn't return their affection, why not even things out with an attractive twenty-one-year-old tutor, Alexei Belyaev, imported into the house to teach the Islayevs' ten-year-old son, Kolya? Of course, Natalya is going to fall in love with him. And he won't love her back. Or will he? This is the dramatic tension in the comedy. Naturally, Natalya needs a rival: seventeen-year-old Vera, the family's ward, taken in as an orphan and so close to marriageable age that a proposal is imminent from Bolshintsov (aged forty-eight), a neighbour and friend of the family doctor Shpigelsky (aged forty). (Turgenev really does give an age to every single person on the cast list. This is either very annoying or very helpful to casting directors.)

More instances of unrequited love are added into the mix so that, in the end, it's a merry-go-round of people sighing over people looking the other way. Islayev and Rakitin love Natalya. She doesn't love them. Natalya and Vera love Belyaev. He probably doesn't love either of them. Bolshintsov loves Vera. She does not love him. Even the servants are caught up in this, Shakespeare-style: the German tutor has an eye for Katya, the maid, who is really not that into him.

Reading this play helped me enormously, as I could see the comedy of my own situation. It's horrible when you love someone madly and they just think you are vaguely tolerable. It's almost worse when they seem to go along with the idea of having a relationship with you (as God's Gift, Son of God's Gift, appeared to do) but they also seem somehow reluctant. An outright *nyet* would be more humane. I could see that it was unenviable and tragic that I had ended up in a relationship with the perfect boyfriend and yet he had entered into this relationship almost as if coerced. And yet somewhere deep inside me, I did realize that it was funny on some level. It was hard to know which one of us was more ridiculous: was it me, loving someone who clearly thought very little of me, or him, wasting his time with an English girlfriend he didn't like that much and who frequently wore an oversized Aran sweater knitted by her Northern Irish grandmother because she thought it made her look like Debbie Harry. (In fact, it made me look like a bag lady. You can see now why the passion of God's Gift, Son of God's Gift, was not ignited.)

Turgenev combines the horror and the comedy of this situation like no one else. *A Month in the Country* has an almost Shakespearean feel, with people running around the birch forest sighing after each other and no one getting what they want. The key focus, though, has to be Rakitin. And Turgenev admitted that this character represented him. There is little in the play to indicate Rakitin's physical state, but you can imagine him making big saucer eyes at Natalya, looking at her like a puppy and generally behaving like a lovesick teenager. (Put him in an oversized Aran sweater and he could be me.) Most of his scenes in the play are with Natalya, so we mostly get to see him almost exclusively in this state, as if he's incapable of existing in any other way. Being the victim of unrequited love defines his identity. In the scenes where Natalya is not present, Rakitin behaves and speaks much more like a normal, rational person. This is Turgenev's idea of self-parody: he knows that love — and especially unrequited love – makes fools of us all. And he knows what it is like to be one of those fools.

Reading the play, I realized that Rakitin's unrequited love is so extreme that it represents the best ever argument for not bothering with this miserable one-sided state. 'You wait!' Rakitin says, in the love rant to his rival Belyaev in the final act of the play. 'You will know what it means to be tied to a petticoat, to be enslaved and poisoned — and how shameful and agonizing that slavery is! . . . You will learn at last how little you get for all your sufferings . . .' We have to remember, of course, that this is a comedy. And it's possible to get a laugh out of Rakitin's condition. But there's also something poignant here. Is this Turgenev talking? Is this how he felt all his life, up against Viardot? If he was writing this character to parody himself or to convince himself to change, he did not succeed. He only wrote this play several years into his acquaintance with Viardot. He had another three decades of it to go.

The reader knows the truth, though, whether about Turgenev or Rakitin. A mysterious force has not tied them to the petticoat. No. They have tied themselves there. And they rather like it. Realizing this made me blush. I also liked loving someone who did not love me that much. It was safe. I knew where I stood. There would be no unpleasant surprises. It was one of those moments where you feel a writer has seen straight into your soul. Your stupid, self-defeating, woolly Aran soul.

Perhaps one of the most astonishing things about Turgenev is just how long he went on being a fool in love. He must have enjoyed it, too. It was virtually his identity, and he seemed to attain some measure of control in being with someone who didn't love him back and was never going to leave her husband. Maybe he liked the predictability of it. That's one of the things about unrequited love (and I know myself well enough to know this is true for me): while it hurts in theory, it also protects you from hurt. When you fall in love with someone and they love you back, there is the chance for disappointment and disillusionment. There is the risk of rejection. With unrequited love, this isn't a problem: you have been rejected before anything has even started. Unrequited love, once discovered, is ultimately an expression of masochism. Maybe it even represents a fear of intimacy. If you're not afraid of intimacy, why not love someone who can love you, too? It's so much easier to be madly in love with someone with whom there is no chance whatsoever of it working out.

Much later on in life, I learned that I needn't have identified with Turgenev so readily. There is no point in feeling sorry for him. Although he was madly in love with the on-off mistress who would never give up her other life for him, this didn't stop him from having plenty of other ladies on the go. Not a bit of it. As Yarmolinsky writes in his biography, Turgenev thought he was a better writer 'when the page was warmed by the glow of a casual affair'. The biographer adds, 'One should approach every woman as a potential mistress: variety, not satisfaction, is what talent feeds upon.' (Yarmolinsky's words, not Turgenev's. But still. Turgenev's relationship with Viardot did not prevent him from having at least one other child with another woman.) Maybe this is where I went wrong. I could have loved God's Gift, Son of God's Gift, and felt tortured and unloved but still had loads of other boyfriends. It did not occur to me for a second that variety might have solved my problem. I would have assumed it would make it worse. That is possibly why I am not a Russian playwright.

The more I learned about Turgenev, though, the more I understood that I very much liked him as a person (despite his philandering, which, I suppose, we must write off as pretty normal for a nineteenth-century aristocratic writer). As well as Pauline Viardot never loving him as much as he wanted, he didn't really get that much love back for his work either. *A Month in the Country* had a reception which can best be described as lukewarm. The great director Stanislavsky called the play 'boring and unstageable' even after he had cast himself in it as Rakitin. How insulting is that? You're in a play you've chosen to stage and you're playing the lead, but you still think the play is awful. This was to be Turgenev's lot in life: never quite appreciated for the talent he had.

However, there was a moment of sublime recognition, and it came during his lifetime. As the biographer and translator Rosamund Bartlett has pointed out, there was a time when Turgenev was known as the one and only great Russian writer. In the 1880s, Turgenev was more popular in translation and more famous a name than Tolstoy. Bartlett quotes from the British literary periodical the *Saturday Review* in 1905: 'We remember mentioning his [Tolstoy's] existence to an American novelist of first rank, a great admirer of Turgenev, who did not seem inclined to believe that people would soon come to realize the greater power of Tolstoy.' The novelist cited was almost certainly Henry James. To underline what is being said here: Turgenev is more worth reading than Tolstoy. That's a pretty good recommendation.

Soon, though, both Tolstoy and Dostoevsky overtook Turgenev's reputation both at home and abroad. When I was first studying Russian in the mid-1990s, he was not fashionable at all, and it was quite by chance that I had picked up a copy of *A Month in the Country* and started reading it: I thought it looked an easy read (and I did not want to read his novel *Fathers and Sons*, which was what was on my reading list). When I was at university, no one particularly liked or approved of Turgenev, even the daffiest of lecturers who were madly in love with Chekhov (also slightly unpopular at the time). It was considered bad form to spend too much time reading him, instead of twentieth-century avant-garde writers. Turgenev was seen as soft and inconsequential.

Nowadays, he is not entirely reviled: he's well known as a dramatist, his plays are popular on stage and adapted for the screen. But he is not what you would call 'up there' for everyone. The seeds for this fate were sown in the latter part of his career, when Turgenev, the writer first known abroad as the one and only voice of Russia, suddenly became seen as 'too Western'. This was code for being too caught up with the aesthetics of the novel and not enough with the moral and spiritual principles of the characters. Virginia Woolf wrote that he was appreciated 'more for his formal artistry than for his political or social commentary'. 'Formal artistry' is code for writing about human nature and the natural world and love and flowers, instead of writing about God and why the serfs should be emancipated. (This was slightly unfair, as Turgenev did believe the serfs should be emancipated and wrote about this, too.) Basically, Turgenev became more closely associated with the style of Henry James, Hemingway and Flaubert. He was supposedly not enough like Tolstoy and Dostoevsky to be properly Russian. This was – and is – both his charm and his downfall.

For someone who comes across in all his biographies as sensitive and mild-mannered, Turgenev is a surprisingly divisive character. Virginia Woolf and Henry James loved him. Tolstoy wasn't sure about him. And Dostoevsky straight up hated him. Nabokov, however, a notoriously plain-speaking critic of other writers, listed him as the fourth most important Russian writer. If you think that's mean and Turgenev should have been placed higher up, please believe me when I say that, coming from

Nabokov, this is the most gigantic compliment you can ever imagine. While listing him as one of the best writers ever, he also sniffed that Turgenev was 'pleasant' but not 'great'. The other writers on the list were Tolstoy, Gogol and Chekhov, in that order. (Dostoevsky would be gutted, I'm sure.)

It's not a recommendation that every writer would necessarily want to receive but, later on, Lenin was a big fan of Turgenev. He loved Turgenev's novel *Spring Torrents*. Lenin supposedly became obsessed with Turgenev's works after the death of his brother, who was reading Turgenev shortly before he died. Lenin's passion for this colourful, aristocratic writer is strange enough in itself: Turgenev was a dandy partial to silk waistcoats and velvet smoking jackets. He spent more time in Europe than he did in Russia, travelling, partying and going to the opera. He spent his whole life devoted to an opera singer who was married to another man. And he is the only Russian author I have come across who was open about having a favourite champagne: Roederer, served with ice. (Now you see why I love him.)

He was also extremely entertaining and eccentric. He once said that the actress Sarah Bernhardt reminded him of a toad. He threw an inkwell at Pauline Viardot one time when she annoyed him. When he was suffering acutely from an undiagnosed severe physical condition, only months away from death, immobile and miserable, he described himself as a 'human oyster'. At the same time, he cheerfully undertook a 'milk cure', which, predictably enough, consisted of drinking nine or ten glasses of milk a day and not much else. He reported that it made him feel much better. He sat in bed and dictated his last short story, entitled, appropriately enough, 'The End'. Later, it turned out that he had cancer of the spinal cord. No amount of milk is going to cure that.

I like to think of Turgenev as being charming and a bit bonkers. He liked to have a good time and make jokes. These were jokes which not everybody understood, and especially not Dostoevsky. Virginia Woolf reviewed a biography of him under the title 'A Giant with Very Small Thumbs'. This was not an unreasonable description. Woolf saw him as a literary giant. And he did have very small thumbs, by his own account, at least. In one account of Turgenev's time in England, Anne Thackeray (eldest daughter of *Vanity Fair* author William Makepeace Thackeray and step-aunt of Virginia Woolf) tells of the time she invited the Russian author to tea and he didn't turn up. 'I am so sorry I could not come,' he said later. 'So very sorry. I was prevented. Look at my thumbs! [. . .] Yes, my thumbs! See how small they are. People with such little thumbs can never do what they intend to do, they always let themselves be prevented.' (Relating this story in *Turgenev and England*, the biographer Patrick Waddington assumes that Turgenev means he was 'prevented' not by his thumbs but by the fact that he was with his mistress.)

Turgenev was a great fan of the nineteenth-century dinner-party custom of interrupting proceedings to ask guests an important question, like 'Who was your first love?', 'Do you believe in God?' or 'Is there life after death?' Turgenev captures one of these dinner-party moments in the opening pages to his 1860 novel, *First Love*, in which the hero, Vladimir Petrovich, answers the question about his first love: 'In my case there was no first love. I began with the second.' Doesn't this sound romantic and intriguing? Ah, Turgenev! But he immediately cuts it down to size: Vladimir says his first love was his nanny, when he was six years old. So she should count as his first love (because he really did love her). But at the same time, she doesn't really count. This is typical Turgenev: appearing to say something profound and philosophical but undercutting it with something light and frothy, trying to make fun of his own hopelessness in matters of the heart.

Tolstoy was always wary of stating too much appreciation for Turgenev, although they had a cautious friendship for most of their lives, with occasional upsets. The two once had a huge falling-out when they disagreed over whether it was a good thing for Turgenev's daughter to take in 'the poor clothing of the paupers' for mending. Turgenev considered this a generous act of charity. Tolstoy thought it was pretentious and hypocritical. Turgenev uttered an unrecorded swear word. There's also a suggestion that Tolstoy disapproved of the illegitimacy of Turgenev's daughter, who was the child of a serf. (Which is silly in itself, as Tolstoy had also fathered a child by a serf, telling his wife about it just before they got married, which upset her immensely, as already discussed.) They later exchanged letters, variously demanding and requesting apologies and culminating in Tolstoy challenging Turgenev to a duel. They both managed to wriggle out of this by sending more letters, and Tolstoy, during one of his religious phases, eventually apologized. Tolstoy wrote that Turgenev 'lives in luxury and idleness' but that he was 'the most likeable of pagans'.

Tolstoy and Turgenev did have some good times together, though, with Turgenev visiting Tolstoy at his estate at Yasnaya Polyana. He was well known among Tolstoy's children for impersonating a chicken while eating soup. When Turgenev visited friends, he would make a great show of checking the two watches he carried at all times, one in the pocket of his (usually dark green velvet) jacket, one in the pocket of his waistcoat. He would get them both out and make certain they showed the same time. There's a sense that he sometimes got a bit carried away with his own japes. He told Tolstoy's children stories about Jules Verne, referring to him as 'a stay-at-home and a frightful bore'. He was also happy to dance for them, just to amuse them, and to amuse himself. That night in his diary, an unimpressed Tolstoy wrote, 'Turgenev's can-can. Sad.'

But Turgenev wasn't really as much of a show-off as he seemed. When unprovoked, he was a modest and reasonable man. In his letters, he writes that, compared to the work of Tolstoy and Dostoevsky, his own pen was like a 'thin squeak'. He was the one who arranged for the translation of *War and Peace* into French and it was he who urged Tolstoy not to give up writing fiction: 'Be warned by my example. Do not let life slip between your fingers. These are the words of a deeply and deservedly unhappy man.' Turgenev wrote this to Tolstoy from his deathbed (presumably surrounded by pints of milk), begging Tolstoy to continue, describing *A Confession*, the extremely depressing essay about spiritual transformation, as 'the gloomiest negation of human life'. (As previously discussed, it's worse than this.) 'My friend, resume your literary work!' he urged, in vain.

Turgenev's argument with Dostoevsky was serious and lasting. It took place in Baden Baden, the spa town that became 'Europe's summer capital' in the mid-nineteenth century. (Even before this time, Russian literary cartoons were fond of depicting Pushkin disappearing to Baden Baden at the faintest slight. 'Right, that's it, I'm going to Baden Baden.') The row between Dostoevsky and Turgenev was mostly about whether it was good to be German and therefore bad to be Russian. It started with a remark Dostoevsky made about Turgenev not understanding Russia because he lived in the West: 'Train your telescope on Russia and examine us, because otherwise it really is hard to make us out.' (For some reason, this always reminds me of Tina Fey doing an impression of Sarah Palin saying, 'I can see Russia from my kitchen.') During this argument, Dostoevsky screamed that the Germans were 'rogues and swindlers'. This so incensed Turgenev that he lost it completely and said, 'You should know that I have settled here permanently and I consider myself a German, not a Russian, and I'm proud of it!' Oh dear.

What was ridiculous about this exchange – which was purely a battle of egos – was that Turgenev himself was prone to railing about how much he hated Europe and wanted to return to

Russia. He wrote that the only decent things in Paris were music, poetry, nature and dogs, and they couldn't even do those properly. (The hunting is 'disgusting'.) He couldn't stand the French: 'Everything that is not theirs seems to them wild and stupid.' The philosopher Isaiah Berlin recalls Turgenev's letters hankering for 'the smells and sights of the Russian autumn': ' . . . bread, wisps of smoke, the sound of the head peasant's boots in the hall'. Dostoevsky never got over his animosity towards Turgenev and caricatured him as the lisping and irritating character of Karmazinov, a pretentious and foppish writer in *The Devils*. In fact, it soon became something of a national literary sport to make fun of Turgenev in your work. Chekhov referred to him in his short 'An Anonymous Story', lampooning his idealistic notions about love.

But despite all this silliness about wanting to be German, Turgenev is essentially lovable, as only a person who loves a woman his whole life who cannot love him back can be. He did not have a happy childhood, and his mother is said to have bullied him. One of my favourite anecdotes about him is the one concerning something that happened to him when he was nineteen. While in Germany, he was travelling on a steamboat that caught fire. During this incident, Turgenev supposedly 'reacted in a cowardly manner', a character flaw that saw him denigrated in Russian high society. This is the perfect example of how easy it was to become an object of ridicule in that tittle-tattle world of nineteenth-century Russian letters. And what a claustrophobic and paranoia-making world that must have been.

In those uncertain times, with everyone bitching about his cowardice and comparing him to new writers like Tolstoy and Dostoevsky, and with Turgenev himself travelling all over Europe, trailing after Pauline Viardot, their relationship, however one-sided, must have seemed like the one constant comfort to him. It made him into a sensitive writer, at least. When an apprentice writer asked Hemingway for reading tips, Turgenev was the only author whose entire oeuvre Hemingway recommended. Virginia Woolf praised his 'generalised and balanced view of life'. It's sometimes hard to work out whether Turgenev was a great comedian with razor-sharp black humour or a manic depressive who portrayed things so blackly that they couldn't help but be funny. One of the first stories he wrote, 'Mumu', is about a deaf and dumb peasant who is forced to kill the one thing he loves the most, his dog, Mumu. If you had to write a parody of a depressed Russian writer's most depressing story, you would write this story.

Turgenev could also be deadly serious. In 'Smoke', one of his best-known stories, he describes life in a way that sounds almost like Tolstoy at his most depressing: 'Everything in the world, and, particularly, in Russia, as well as everything a man does, is just a puff of smoke which disappears without a trace without achieving anything.' Quick, pass the Roederer before he expands on this. In many ways, Turgenev's life lessons can be said to be as frustrating as those of Tolstoy. Isaiah Berlin wrote of Turgenev: 'He knew the Russian reader wanted to be told what to believe and how to live.' (Yes, please, we would like this, too! We are waiting for the great message of wisdom! Bestow it upon us!) But he wasn't going to give them what they wanted, he adds. 'Problems are raised and, for the most part, left unanswered.' Oh, thanks a lot, Turgenev. Thanks a lot. Go back to your sad can-can.

That said, although Turgenev is no better at offering definitive answers than Tolstoy, he is unmatched in his ability to describe the tragicomic reality of certain situations. And just by portraying things as they really are, he shows the truth about life more clearly than any piece of well-meant advice. I'm not sure I was directly influenced by *A Month in the Country* to take the course of action I took that summer in Odessa. But it must have played some part. There are several scenes of confrontation in the play where the person who is tragically in love decides to challenge the object of their affections directly. It is the moment of the greatest folly and the purest bravery. It is the moment of ultimate knowledge: love me or reject me. It was a moment I decided would happen on a beach in Odessa.

I was coming to the end of my time in Ukraine (where I was on holiday, at the end of my university year abroad in Russia) and would soon be facing my return to England. I needed to know whether God's Gift, Son of God's Gift, wanted to be with me or not. I wanted a commitment or, at the very least, an indication. I would settle for some small sign of non-coerced physical passion. Most Saturday nights, we would hang out on the beach with a group of people drawn from the band and its many hangers-on. The alcohol would run out at around 10 p.m. and the party would move on to someone's house. That night, I made sure it ran out more quickly than usual, by drinking as much of it as possible myself and discreetly pouring away plastic cupfuls of *portvein* ('port wine' – actually more like cough syrup) into the sand. Soon the cry went up for beer, and most of the party headed up the sand dunes to the alcohol kiosk.

'*Ostanem'sya. Razdenem'sya*,' I said, in the direction of God's Gift, Son of God's Gift – 'Let us remain here and undress ourselves.' As soon as the last straggler had disappeared out of sight over the sand dunes, I began to take my clothes off. I had decided. On this night, I would not be English or Russian or anything. I would be myself. And I would do something reckless, just because I felt like doing it. (And also because I was really quite drunk.) I left my clothes in a neat pile on a slope above the waves and ran screaming into the foam – just as I remembered that I never went swimming in Odessa because the water was too polluted. When the water got up to my belly button, I started as something floated past me. It was an ice-cream wrapper printed with the word 'Eskimo'. 'My reading speed in Cyrillic is equal to my reading speed in English now,' I thought to myself, pleased.

Before my shoulders were under I turned back – God's Gift, Son of God's Gift, was long gone, miles away up the beach. Unrequited love is painful and humiliating. Avoid it at all costs if you possibly can, while acknowledging that it's almost impossible to avoid. Sometimes, we have to do stupid things, because we are inherently foolish. If Tolstoy had been around to write in his diary that day, he would have put: 'Viv's skinny-dip. Sad.'

5. How to Not be Your Own Worst Enemy: *Eugene Onegin* by Alexander Pushkin
(Or: Don't kill your best friend in a duel)

'Bliss was near, so altogether/unattainable . . .'

You cannot be a student of the Russian language without encountering Pushkin at some point. And most Russian teachers will want you to learn him off by heart and weep and wail and gnash your teeth as you recite his words while mournfully waving a handkerchief soaked in the blood of your enemy whom you have just shot in a duel. Because to know Pushkin is to know the ways of the duel. By some estimates, he fought in as many as twenty-nine duels. Which was apt, because most of the time when I first read his work, under duress, I really wished that someone would shoot me. The lesson of Pushkin is: don't be an idiot. This is ironic, because Pushkin himself more or less died of being an idiot. He barely needed all these other foes who wanted to challenge him. He was already his own worst enemy. (He was shot in an arguably unnecessary and ego-driven duel.)

Eugene Onegin is the classic starting point for Pushkin. It's about a man who is the author of his own misfortune. Eugene Onegin metaphorically shoots himself in the foot (before eventually non-metaphorically shooting his best friend) by not realizing that a woman who is madly in love with him is his soulmate. Instead, he spurns her. Later he understands, and thinks, 'Doh.' I'll be honest: it took me a long time to get into it. For many years, not even the four-page digression on the beauty of women's feet at the ball did it for me. ('. . . dear ladies' feet fly past like hail . . . I love their feet . . . my little feet, where have you vanished . . . to lie down at her feet like slaves! . . . to smother her dear feet with kissing . . .') This is a very famous bit, known in academic circles solemnly as 'the pedal digression'. It all builds up to Pushkin's idea of a punchline: 'But now I've praised the queens of fashion, enough of my loquacious lyre: they don't deserve what they inspire in terms of poetry or passion – their looks and language in deceit are just as nimble as . . . their feet.' Whether all that was worth four pages, I'm not sure. But I'm glad he gave it a go. You can tell from this tiny extract from the stanzas about the ball in Chapter 1 that this is the most classical of all classical works; it's more like reading Homer than Tolstoy. We are not talking beach read here.

An early brush with Pushkin had put me off even before I knew anything about him. Two years before the skinny-dipping incident and long before anyone had thought to name me Dearest Teeny Tiny Little VIP, I arrived at university to learn Russian, unable to speak a word of the language. This was normal. I was not supposed to know how to speak Russian at this point. I was learning 'from scratch' with dozens of other students. Most of us spoke at least two other languages and were used to traditional language teaching. We were expecting vocabulary lists and perhaps a bit of role play. Instead, the first lesson I ever had in Russian featured a video of a parrot squawking the tongue-twister-like words: *Priatno poznakomit'sya!* ('Pleased to meet you!') These words were difficult enough to repeat already, without trying to understand them spoken by a parrot.

I was perturbed by this teaching method. I did not want to learn how to speak like a parrot. I wanted to learn to speak like a Russian. Surely this was like teaching someone English and starting with 'Pretty Polly'? To this day, I struggle to keep a straight face when I say, 'Pleased to meet you' to anyone in Russian, as I feel like squawking in their face, twitching my beak and shedding some feathers, just to show I'm getting it right.

A few weeks after we had graduated from the parrot video, though, we moved on to Pushkin. If I thought the parrot was a bad idea, this was an even worse one. It's like giving someone a two-week course in English and then saying, 'And now we're going to read *Othello*.' It's fairly typical of the teaching of Russian, though. They like to throw you in at the deep end. And they like to make sure you remain completely intimidated by the language for as long as possible. That way, if you pass on to the other side and actually do learn to speak it, you'll maintain the age-old myth that it's difficult to learn and pass that on to other people so that the Russian speakers can remain in their own special and secret club. Having to read Pushkin several weeks into a 'Russian from scratch' course is a sort of hazing you never recover from. It is specially designed to make you want to haze others so that they will suffer as you have suffered. To quote Pushkin: 'I want to understand you. I study your obscure language.' Gulp.

What we were taught in the non-Pushkin lessons was not hugely practical as it was, and we were largely expected to pick up as much vocabulary as possible by ourselves. On one occasion, we had a word test and I scored one mark out of a possible fifty. For someone who had prided herself on her language skills at school, barely dropping a mark for years, this was horrific and shaming. (So much so that, when I was at school, people used to joke that if I got 99 per cent in an exam, it wasn't because I had got any of the answers wrong, it was simply because I had spelled my own name wrong. Which, knowing my name, was entirely probable.) The one word I did get right, though, was the most important word on the test as far as I was concerned. I turned out to be the only person in the class who knew the word for 'towel'. I continued to limit my learning to things I found useful or entertaining. Later, in one oral test, I told the examiners my Ukrainian boyfriend's grandmother had told me I needed fattening up because I had an arse like a sparrow. If I could say things like this, I reasoned, what did I need Pushkin for?

The struggle, though, was deeply humiliating. All the rest of that first academic year of learning Russian, I felt like I was floundering. I never managed to finish the Pushkin poem we were reading ('The Bronze Horseman'). And I ended the year with the worst results I'd ever had in any test, barely scraping a pass. The day I got the results I was back home at my parents' house in Somerset. I locked myself in the bathroom and cried. But although I had been brought low, somewhere deep inside I knew I was never going to be defeated again. Looking back, I think my initial frustration with myself at failing to live up to the standards of this ambitious teaching method ('Week One: learn two words of Russian parrot talk . . . Week Four: Pushkin') was one of the reasons I later became obsessed with Russian and with learning it perfectly. That bloody parrot made me even more determined to be properly Russian.

When I initially encountered *Eugene Onegin*, then, I held it at one remove, still biased by the avian-influenced exam failure and convinced that this was just a stuffy story about aristocratic romance. For students of Russian who first encounter this novel, there's a joke about the pronunciation: 'You might need One Gin to get through it. Or you might need two.' (Oh, how we laughed.) I turned to his work willingly much later, because I wanted more insight into this idea of the Russian soul. And it is widely recognized that Pushkin is the place to go looking for that. Not only is his work seen as the purest expression of the Russian language, he is seen as the person who expresses better than anyone else what it means to be Russian. Plus, to be honest, by avoiding Pushkin, you really are creating more work for yourself with Russians. They will expect you to know about him. And they will regard you as an enemy if you don't.

The language of Pushkin is a truly wondrous thing and has no need of all the 'Keep Out, Idiots!' signs that academics seem to want to erect on this turf. What makes it so special? The same qualities Shakespeare has in English: a mastery of the language that feels rich and exciting; a mix of simple and original expressions that sound as fresh as when they were first written, centuries ago; and a sense of musicality. I like the themes of his work most of all, though: the tragedy of guilt in *Boris Godunov*, the dangers of greed in *The Queen of Spades*, the threat of hubris in *Ruslan and Ludmila*. The most attractive quality is the quiet beauty of his fatalism, which feels very Russian but somehow also very human and universal. From the 1821 poem, 'I Have Outlasted All Desire':

> I have outlasted all desire,
> My dreams and I have grown apart,
> My grief alone is left entire,
> The gleamings of an empty heart.

How could you write lines like this and not be a simply marvellous person?

I sometimes wonder if most of the reason a lot of people hold Russian literature in such awe is because of Pushkin. Seen from afar, his work can seem off-putting to anyone who isn't an academic or a Russian specialist. Not least because he is widely regarded as completely untranslatable (something which, weirdly, no one seems to say about Shakespeare, who must be a total nightmare to translate). Pushkin is the ultimate Russian literary snob's author. 'Oh, you can't read Russian? Oh well, there's no point in you reading Pushkin, then. You just wouldn't get it.' This makes me sigh and heave a little. If anyone is ever telling you that you can't 'get' something because you lack some kind of intelligence, they are usually telling you something about themselves.

The easy part of *Eugene Onegin* is the plot, which is genius. Eugene Onegin, a foppish and slightly irritating artistic type, inherits his uncle's estate. He moves to the country and meets Tatyana, who is a highly impressionable young woman. She falls hopelessly in love with him and writes him a letter in French revealing her love. He more or less laughs at her and casts her aside. Meanwhile, he does another terrible thing. While he's at a name-day party, he allows himself to get into a situation where he makes his best friend Lensky jealous of the attention he is paying to Lensky's intended, Tatyana's sister, Olga. This situation gets out of hand when, really, there was no need (Onegin has no feelings for Olga), and Lensky challenges Onegin to a duel. Lensky is killed. Distraught and guilty, Onegin leaves the country.

Several years later, Onegin returns to St Petersburg from abroad and attends a ball. He finds himself in the company of Tatyana, who has married an older man, a general. Looking at her through more mature eyes, Onegin realizes that he is madly in love with her and declares himself. But, of course, Tatyana is a moral person, and there is no chance. Onegin has ruined both their lives with his idiocy and they can never be happy. Tatyana at least has the comfort of the moral high ground and of knowing that she was right. Onegin has made his bed and he has to lie in it, alone. (I am speaking metaphorically. It doesn't end with him in bed on his own, crying, although it should do. And I hope no one else goes in his bed ever again.)

There are echoes here of the fastidiousness that we see about age in *Anna Karenina* and *A Month in the Country*. It's easy to look at *Eugene Onegin* and think that it's about an age gap: Onegin is the 'older man' who spurns a young girl. In fact, Tatyana is most likely seventeen, possibly eighteen or nineteen. Onegin is twenty-five. She is sometimes represented as a schoolgirl but, in fact, setting her cap at Onegin was an entirely realistic thing to do. He is the one who gets the timing wrong and disregards her. Despite being the older of the two, by the time he is mature enough to know what he should have done, he has missed his chance. This is *Eugene Onegin*'s message about life: we are foolish and we don't know what's good for us until it's too late. Not only is life difficult and unpredictable but, often, we miss opportunities to grab our greatest chance at happiness. And we have only ourselves to blame. (Sorry. But, as previously stated, I did not guarantee that all these life lessons were going to be cheery. Most of them aren't, as you will already have worked out.)

Eugene Onegin is known as a classic of Russian literature, an early prototype for the prose novel and the epitome of the theme of the 'superfluous man', Russia's answer to the Byronic hero, a man with wealth and privilege who doesn't know what to do with his life. It is a strange and difficult piece. I'm sure pedants would argue that you must read it as a text and that seeing it on stage doesn't count. But, for me, it wasn't until I saw a Russian production at the Barbican in London that everything changed and I finally understood Pushkin's message and felt engaged and excited by the story. The theatre was showing a Russian production by Moscow's Vakhtangov Theatre. My appreciation of this production was very possibly influenced by an accident that occurred in the bar shortly before the performance started. I was at the theatre alone because I was reviewing the play for a radio programme. I arrived relatively early and, being someone who rarely goes to the Barbican, I decided to investigate the eating and drinking offerings of this cultural venue. I soon found a bar that served what looked like the most inventive cocktails, including one that featured a favourite ingredient, lavender. Very possibly, it was a martini bar and so a lavender martini. I ordered this drink. When it arrived, I drank it, and it was delicious. About halfway through drinking it, I thought to myself, 'This is lovely, but it tastes nothing like lavender.' It was the wrong drink. I looked at the bartender. 'I'm really sorry,' I said, 'I know I've drunk most of this, but I've just realized it's not what I ordered. I wanted the lavender one.' He rightly judged that it was not worth arguing with someone who had just drunk half a cocktail far too quickly and made me the lavender one. And so I drank it. (I can't remember now what the other drink was. They were both equally delicious.) All this is to say that, by the time I sat down to watch *Eugene Onegin*, I was in an extremely receptive mood. This was an example of someone accidentally being the author of their own good fortune (which is the opposite of what happens in Onegin).

It was a gorgeous production, carefully themed, with all the women wearing white or pastel costumes, the odd minstrel dashing across the stage carrying a balalaika and Tatyana, the heroine of the piece, waltzing with a giant stuffed bear. (At this point, I began to wonder if I had had a third or even a fourth cocktail that I had forgotten about.) It was very long, this play, nearly three and a half hours, but it passed as if I were in a dream. By the end, Russians in the audience were weeping into their furs, applauding wildly, screaming, 'Bravo!' and throwing flowers on to the stage, which is entirely normal and low-key behaviour for a Russian theatre audience.

This production used a clever device that helped me to understand that Eugene Onegin's biggest regret is his lack of self-awareness: he thwarted himself. The play brought this out by having two actors play Onegin on stage at the same time. One depicted him as an arrogant young man; the other, an older actor, could look at his younger self with frustration and self-loathing. It was a powerful depiction of hindsight. Pushkin's story is one about life's failure to align with our greatest hopes and dreams. It's an illustration of wrong time, wrong place. It's about the tendency we all have to act against our own best interests, not to know what's good for us. Just as Tolstoy is empathetic about not blaming his characters for behaving as they do, Pushkin lets Onegin off the hook: we all behave in ways which damage us sometimes. We just can't help it. But maybe watching someone else do it will save us from repeating the error.

Not long after I saw that Vakhtangov Theatre production, I saw the opera *Eugene Onegin* at the Royal Opera House, a production directed by Kasper Holten. On this occasion, what struck me most was not so much Tatyana's passion or Onegin's mournful regret but the disaster that is Lensky, Onegin's best friend. The Lensky storyline is a subplot. The real focus is on the love story between Onegin and Tatyana. But, in reality, Onegin's behaviour towards Lensky is even more offensive and idiotic than his behaviour towards Tatyana. When he loses her, the only person he really hurts is himself. With Lensky, he behaves recklessly and his actions result in Lensky's death. In this production, at the duel, Lensky is struck down and killed. He then lies there, in full view of the audience, for the entirety of the production, while all the other actors walk around him, ignoring his corpse. I found this extremely poignant (not to mention extremely annoying for the actor in question, who later said that he found it very uncomfortable and difficult to breathe, bless him). Perhaps the strangest part was when Onegin and Tatyana sing regretfully at each other towards the end, never glancing down at Lensky, who is still lying dead near the stalls.

For me this was a metaphor for life. When you get things badly wrong and act against your own best interests, you may well find yourself face to face with the corpse of Lensky at all times. And no matter how much time passes or how much you move on, he's always lying there, waiting to remind you of what a stupid idiot you are. Onegin truly is his own worst enemy: he kills his best friend and has to drag his ghost around for the rest of his life. And, on top of this, he has laughed in the face of the woman who should have become his wife. This is a wonderful and useful life lesson about taking responsibility and acknowledging when you are being a complete fool. It always reminds me of the line in the film *When Harry Met Sally* when Carrie Fisher as Marie says: 'You'll have to spend the rest of your life knowing that someone else is married to your husband.' *Eugene Onegin* is about spending the rest of your life knowing that someone else is married to your wife and you have killed your best friend.

I wish there were more opportunities to draw parallels between the works of Pushkin and the screenplays of Nora Ephron. But instead, Pushkin's reputation just seems to become more obscure and elitist as time goes on. This seems a real shame, as Pushkin the man was a fascinating, appealing and complex character. And, just as with Shakespeare, his work is hilarious, complicated, wise. The question is this: how do you get to all that painlessly? Of all the authors in this book, he's probably the most difficult to persuade people to read. (His only real competition is Solzhenitsyn, whose work, largely because of its subject matter, is by definition heavy and difficult.) Sadly, for too long, the appreciation of Pushkin has been reserved for pedants and intellectuals, something I partly blame on Vladimir Nabokov, another candidate for the title of 'greatest Russian writer of all time' (at least in his own mind). There can be no bigger pedant or intellectual than Nabokov. His 1964 translation of *Eugene Onegin*, the painstaking work of a lifetime, put off a whole other generation, underlining Pushkin's reputation as 'untranslatable' and unreachable for anyone who isn't a) Russian or b) an academic.

It's not surprising that Nabokov undertook to produce the

most accurate translation so far of Pushkin's great work. It's a huge challenge, and Nabokov wanted to be the one to prove that he was up to it and could do it better than anyone else. He also conceived the project in part as revenge on a previous translation which he judged 'embarrassing' (Walter Arndt's, still widely judged one of the best). This led to what was dubbed 'the biggest literary spat of the 1960s' with Nabokov's friend the critic Edmund Wilson rising to the defence of poor Walter Arndt, and Nabokov and Wilson falling out irrevocably. Although this spat is an indication of the idiocy surrounding the obsession with how special and important Pushkin is, I love every detail of it, and I am thankful for its existence, as it has given me even more reasons to champion *Eugene Onegin* and fight back against the demented pedantry that was ignited by this argument.

This literary quarrel is brilliantly catalogued in Alex Beam's book *The Feud*. (If you still really cannot face the thought of reading Pushkin, please do read this book instead. It is so entertaining.) Cringing and cracking up by turns, Beam recounts the fight between Wilson and Nabokov over the *Onegin* translation, a fight which played itself out in the pages of a number of American literary journals. It didn't have huge global resonance, except perhaps in certain literary circles or in academia. But I do think, one way or another, it became a backdrop to how we think about Russian literature. I can't help but feel that the fallout from this unedifying dogfight between two intensely intelligent but ridiculously pompous men has subconsciously informed a lot of people's reactions to Russian literature over the past fifty years. If these two think Pushkin is impossible to understand and are prepared to ditch a lifelong friendship over it, what hope for the rest of us?

The argument between Wilson and Nabokov, who were great friends for over twenty years before this incident, exemplifies all the worst stereotypes about Russian literature. That it's only for the select few who are 'intelligent enough' to understand it. That it's best not to try to understand it if you don't read Russian fluently. That there's no point in reading it at all if you don't read the perfect translation. All this stuff came up. Worst of all? If you hold an opinion on these books, you will be shot down in flames by others who are better read and more intelligent than you are. So best to stay away, really. The irony is, the two of them were behaving exactly like academic versions of Eugene Onegin: cutting their noses off to spite their faces and throwing a relationship under a bus just to take the moral high ground over the translation of a few nouns.

To be fair on Nabokov, he had every reason and every right to translate *Eugene Onegin*, widely seen as 'the first Russian novel'. You can see why Nabokov might have been annoyed by Walter Arndt's translation; he felt it did the original a disservice. In Arndt's translation, there were, admittedly, some liberties taken. According to Nabokov's account, at one point a husband is mistaken for a lover and an arrow is rendered as a gun. The opening line, 'My uncle has most honest principles', comes out as 'My uncle, decorous old prune.' Clearly, this is about more than just being pedantic. (Although, personally, I would be totally up for reading a poem about an old prune.) But these small differences of opinion (surely the translator's version of 'alternative facts') render Nabokov apoplectic and cause him to embark upon the translation to end all translations, which runs to four volumes and 1,850 pages. This is not quite as long as *War and Peace*, but it's quite an achievement if you consider that the most popular version of *Eugene Onegin* is around two hundred pages. So Nabokov has added 1,650 pages of footnotes. That is a hell of a lot of footnotes. It is quite possibly the biggest act of pedantry in the history of literature.

Nabokov's translation was completely skewered in Edmund

Wilson's review in *The New York Times*, which pointed out that the following words don't really exist in English (or, if they ever did, they are now more or less obsolete): rememorating, producement, curvate, habitude, rummers, familistic, gloam, dit, shippon and scrab. (And you thought Russian seemed like a difficult language.) In the final nail in the coffin of their friendship, Wilson criticizes Nabokov's translation of a line of Russian that reads 'Shall I ever see you again?' Nabokov has it as 'Shall I see you?', which Wilson says sounds like 'the products of those computers which are supposed to translate Russian into English'. It's hard to know at this point which of these two great men comes across as the bigger twit. While all these academic arguments are vastly entertaining, they do discourage 'normal' readers (i.e. people who are not deranged, pedantic Russophiles). And this is deeply unfair, because *Eugene Onegin* is so important in understanding the novel as a literary form. Aside from anything else, it is significant because it serves as a prototype for so much Russian literature that came after. It's the first 'novel' (even though it's in verse). And the character of Tatyana is also important as a type: she provides inspiration for Dostoevsky's Dunya, the 'good' sister of Raskolnikov in *Crime and Punishment*, as well as for Natasha in Tolstoy's *War and Peace*.

It's in Onegin that we first encounter this particular 'type' beloved of Russian fiction: the superhero Byronic man (I am very proud of this Nabokovian wordplay; please applaud) who is above ordinary social and moral norms. Many critics have argued that there is no big message in the book. In my favourite edition, Professor Michael Basker agrees with this to some extent, although he also adds in his introduction: 'It discloses a more serious preoccupation with how best to accommodate to the difficult task of living within life's many vicissitudes and constraints'. That's a mouthful. In other words: it's about exactly what Dostoevsky and Tolstoy are about – how to live a decent life, what to do with your life, how to be a good person. It's a heavily rhymed and metred version of an early self-help book.

I'm not sure Pushkin would have cared about any of this, though. He led a fairly reckless sort of life, not unlike Eugene Onegin's. He courted disaster and loved risk. He was the sort of person who wasn't afraid to do the sorts of things that, further down the line, are likely to make you think, 'Oh, for goodness' sake, why did I do that?' He was completely obsessed by duels, because they were about a) defending his manly honour and b) proving that he was right. He was a social climber, a gambler and a womanizer prone to irrational rages. But love or loathe Pushkin, there is no denying that he is the most extraordinary storyteller (who loved fairy tales, magic and folklore – think J. K. Rowling), the best kind of fantasist, with melodramatic thespian qualities (think the Shakespeare who wrote the sonnets); perhaps, in modern times, he's someone we would even call something of a drama queen (think Oscar Wilde): Pushkin's biographer T. J. Binyon describes the great writer recounting the personal betrayal that led to his death 'as if he were narrating a drama or a novelette that had absolutely nothing to do with him'.

Pushkin was born in 1799 to a family of minor nobility and fading grandeur and it would be difficult to find anyone in Russia at the time with a more exotic background. His great-grandfather on his mother's side was an African prince, kidnapped as a gift for Peter the Great, most probably from the country we now know as Chad. That man went on to become a general and the Tsar's adopted godson, and Pushkin later started a work about his great-grandfather's life entitled 'The Negro of Peter the Great'.

Apart from his increasingly prodigious literary output, I love the characterization of Pushkin as otherwise leading 'a reckless and generally non-productive life'. The best kind of life, surely? He loved to gamble. He loved to drink. He loved women and regularly transferred his affections from one to another. 'All women are charming,' he wrote. 'But the love of men makes them beautiful.' Yet he also maintained childlike qualities throughout his life: he used to graffiti his work with doodles and sketches, he picked wild strawberries in the forests at Zakharovo, the estate an hour west of Moscow where his grandmother had an orchard; in pictures, we see him with messy hair, the collar on his shirt rakishly raised, always with the wrinkled jacket, Byronesque, dishevelled, beautifully tragic. As the biographer Serena Vitale has written, he often had a button trailing off his jacket, a detail that always makes me wish he had spent more time learning needlecraft and less time challenging people to duels.

Pushkin's marriage to Natalia Goncharova, known as the most beautiful woman in all of Russia – she was seventeen, he was thirty-one – was seen as ill-fated from their wedding day. It had been postponed for months because of a cholera epidemic, and the day itself was blighted by signs regarded as bad omens: a wedding ring accidentally dropped, candles mysteriously blowing out during the ceremony. During their first few months of married life in Moscow, though, Pushkin was, for once, content: 'I am married and happy,' he wrote. 'My only wish is that nothing will change.' Shortly afterwards, however, the newlyweds left for St Petersburg, with Pushkin writing: 'I do not like Moscow life. You live here not as you want to live, but as old women want you to.'

What happened when they returned to St Petersburg was a nightmare for Pushkin. The Tsar granted him an honorary but ridiculous and humiliating title – *kammerjunker*; 'junior gentleman of the chamber' – purely so that it would be appropriate for his wife to attend court. She had already caught the eye of the Tsar, as well as that of other admirers. Natalia was described as beautiful and a favourite at court, but she also had a reputation for being uneducated and rather vulgar.

By this time, Pushkin had written *Eugene Onegin*, which he began in 1824 and completed in 1831. The novel itself is weirdly prophetic, or perhaps just brilliantly evocative of the mores of the time. There was a terrible echo of Pushkin's work in the (incredibly stupid) circumstances that led to his death. In real life, Pushkin ended up in exactly Lensky's situation. Pushkin's wife flirted (probably innocuously) with a young officer called George d'Anthès. An anonymous letter was sent to Pushkin, admitting him to 'The Serene Order of Cuckolds'. Pushkin was then more or less obliged to challenge d'Anthès to a duel. Pushkin was shot and died two days later at the age of thirty-seven. D'Anthès never really apologized or showed any sign that he was sorry. But, then, these entirely pointless duels were happening a lot in those days, as Pushkin himself knew. In fact, the only thing that is perhaps not that true to life in *Eugene Onegin* is that Onegin is tortured by having killed his best friend in a duel and never recovers from it. In real life, men were forced to get over this the whole time and didn't beat themselves up about it.

Eugene Onegin reads, then, as an entertaining diversion, a tragic love story and the confession of someone who realizes they have been a complete and utter dolt. As Onegin writes to Tatyana:

> From all sweet things that gave me pleasure
> since then I wrenched my heart aside;
> freedom and peace in substitution
> for happiness, I sought, and ranged
> unloved, and friendless, and estranged,
> What folly! and what retribution!

Awaiting her reply and hoping for the best, Onegin reads Rousseau and Fontenelle, but the only thing he can see in his mind's eye is the letter that Tatyana sent him as a young girl, the letter he laughed at. Tatyana has her chance now to reject him, and we leave Onegin with his heart plunged 'into a raving ocean'. How not to be your own worst enemy? Avoid hubris. Stay humble. Keep an eye out for self-defeating behaviours. Don't duel. And when a very beautiful and intelligent woman sends you a declaration of love, think very, very hard before rejecting it and laughing in her face. Because, one day, she will be the one laughing in yours.

6. How to Overcome Inner Conflict: *Crime and Punishment* by Fyodor Dostoevsky
(Or: Don't kill old ladies for money)

'To go wrong in one's own way is better
than to go right in someone else's.'

Whatever you're going through in life, you don't have it as bad as Raskolnikov, the student who believes he is capable of great things and attempts to, er, prove it to himself by killing the elderly pawnbroker Alyona Ivanovna with an axe and finishing her half-sister off, too. This is a book about how easy it is to convince yourself of things that are a) quite untrue and b) quite mad. If Eugene Onegin has an overly developed sense of entitlement, Raskolnikov feels so insecure that he will do anything to raise his status. Pushkin's greatest work is about blithely destroying your own chance at happiness. Dostoevsky's is about those moments in life when you know you're about to do something very wrong but you do it anyway. *Crime and Punishment* is also predominantly a warning about the dangers of getting too hungry. Raskolnikov always copes with his inner conflict particularly badly when he has not had enough pies to eat.

I often thought of Raskolnikov the year I was living in St Petersburg, as I was near a lot of the places Dostoevsky mentions in the book. My route to the English-language school where I taught went through Sennaya Ploshchad (Haymarket), one of the novel's main settings. Raskolnikov sets out from his rented lodgings here when his mind is tormented by thoughts of murder and he is finally on his way to commit the deed. Coincidentally, when I was there, I found a purveyor of the most superb pies, an old lady who used to set up shop outside the metro with cabbage *pirozhki* which she would keep in a metal bucket, warmed underneath by hot coals. I would buy a few of these hot little pies and munch wistfully on them as I walked along the same canals where Raskolnikov once roamed. At the time, I had an inner conflict of my own: how could I become more Russian but still be English at the same time? The longer I spent in Russia and the more I immersed myself, the more I could feel my identity splitting. I was not inspired to commit murder during my time wandering these streets (although I occasionally wanted to when I was kerb-crawled by all manner of creeps, something that happened on a regular basis at that particular time, as if it had become some sort of fashionable pastime), but I was still gripped with delusions about Russianness which reached almost Raskolnikov levels of insanity. I became more and more convinced of the idea that I had a 'Russian soul'. In my defence, I was high on the exoticism of my temporarily adopted homeland and, being young and naive, low on self-awareness. I did eventually overcome my obsession with speaking exclusively Russian for a period of several months (something I insisted on doing to maintain the 'purity' of my Russian – what a lummox), just in time to realize that it would be a good idea if I got some work experience at the English-language newspaper the *St Petersburg Press*. I thought this would be a good way to incorporate the two halves of me: I could interview people in Russian and write up the interviews in English. That way, I could be both my old self and my new self at the same time. I worked there for a few months in the spring before the summer of the disastrous skinny-dip.

This newspaper was a peculiar set-up, a magnet for expats who were passing through and for young people like me who thought they wanted to be journalists. I wrote articles about rock bands (including about the band of God's Gift, Son of God's Gift). I reviewed restaurants, which often served really terrible food; this wasn't especially mentioned or acknowledged in the 'reviews' because we wanted to make it seem as if St Petersburg was a great place to live (partly because we were busy convincing ourselves). The big scoop that came in when I was there was a picture exclusive provided by a young American photographer who had managed to get a snap of the ultra-nationalist politician Vladimir Zhirinovsky wearing only his Y-fronts (greyish white, wrinkly, much like the man himself) and a pair of roller skates. It caused a scandal in the office. I can't remember whether we published the photograph or not. I have a terrible feeling we did.

My first assignment at this newspaper happened to channel a Dostoevskian idea of nightmarish self-delusion and was a study in the art of inner conflict. I was sent to interview one of the head clowns at the circus. He was a sad, sweet man, with real-life fuzzy clown hair and a mournful, expressive face. The circus was a big deal: a tourist attraction that was on year round but regularly had new performers they wanted to publicize. This man was one of them. He had a message for the world via me, his long-awaited interviewer. He was not a clown. He was so much more than that.

He had pioneered an act that was unique: he had a troupe of performing hedgehogs. He had travelled the world with this act ('Las Vegas, Tokyo . . .') and was keen to impress on me that he was 'no longer a clown'. This was because of his great international success as a renowned animal trainer, which is evidently one step up from being a mere clown. The whole interview was conducted as if he were making some kind of public statement about the end of his previous career. I took it very seriously. I can still see him shaking his head insistently, as he corrected me. 'So when you started out as a clown . . .' '*Ya ne klon* . . . [I'm not a clown]' 'Oh, yes, I'm so sorry . . . So, er, when you became a clown . . .' '*Ya ne klon* . . . [I'm not a clown].'

His act was amazing. Hedgehogs would come and go on his command. They were hedgehogs he had caught himself in the wild and spent months domesticating. He taught them to run around and jump over each other (with the help of various strategically placed ramps). During the finale of his show, he would put a hedgehog in one end of a tube and it would come out as a porcupine at the other. One of his greatest challenges in life, he sighed, was getting the porcupine to stay in the tube (which was like a sort of a tunnel) during the show. This had taken a lot of training. This non-clown really was an extraordinary character. They were extraordinary hedgehogs. And I was very pleased with my scoop. (And with my Russian, which, as you can tell from the content of this hedgehog-based conversation, was now quite advanced.)

When I got back to the office and wrote up my copy, I was called into the editor's office. Editor: 'Why do you keep saying in the copy that he is not a clown?' Me: 'Because he was at great pains to point out that he's not a clown. He is a world-renowned animal trainer. He would be very upset if I didn't say explicitly that he isn't a clown.' Editor: 'But look at the picture.' The circus had supplied a picture of this man posing alongside the hedgehogs and the no longer recalcitrant porcupine. He was wearing a massive fright wig, a Pierrot costume, full-face make-up and a red nose. I paused. 'Yeah. I guess he pretty much looks like a clown.' Editor: 'You need to take out the stuff about him not being a clown.'

I nodded, reluctantly. I got the point. No story makes sense if it contradicts what's in front of your face. On the other hand, in his own eyes, this guy was not a clown. The moral of this story is, I suppose: if you are not a clown, do not dress up as a clown. Or, in other words, sometimes other people can see more clearly who you are than you can. You might want to pretend to be something you're not, but, even if you can't see through it, other people can. You can tell them as many times as you want that you're not a clown, but, if you look like a clown, people will assume you are a clown. This is one of the most painful lessons in life. We all believe things about ourselves that are not true. Usually, these things reflect unresolved inner conflict. Often, we are not aware of them. Other people can see them from a mile off.

When things like the clown encounter happened, it seemed as if Russia was flaunting its madness. One incident occurred around the corner from the huge bookstore Dom Knigi, a place which in itself was slightly mad. This store was a joke among Russian-language students because its name translates as 'House of Book' (rather than 'House of Books', which would be 'Dom Knig'). No one was ever able to tell me properly why it was called House of Book instead of House of Books, but we liked to imagine that it had been named that in the Soviet era in case there was only ever one book on sale. That way, customers could only be pleasantly surprised if there was more than one. Hence the expectation-managing name, House of Book. Funnily enough, House of Book was usually extremely well stocked and contained many exciting items which could be bought for pennies (or, rather, kopecks, while they still existed) in the early 1990s. It also sold postcards with crazy Soviet cartoons on them, one of which featured a bear emerging from a *matryoshka* carrying the slogan: UNEXPECTABLE RUSSIA. Over the course of that year, Russia became a place where I saw terrible and mad things and often barely registered them, or considered them to be completely normal. If someone told me they weren't a clown, even though they dressed in a clown costume, I nodded and believed them. One day on a walk to my English classes near the House of Book, I saw a small bear sitting in the passenger seat of a Lada. I swear it was wearing a seat belt. The only explanation for this bear being there was that it was from the circus. Maybe it was taking a break from the porcupine and his friends.

St Petersburg itself also had a quality about it that could only be termed 'unexpectable' and, occasionally, sinister. You absorbed it and just got used to it. No one has channelled this feeling of menace and magic better than Dostoevsky, who used the city as a backdrop for the ideas that prefigured all the twentieth-century psychological thinking about the unconscious and the subconscious. There are no bears in the front seats of Ladas in his work, but there are lots of weird things in places where they shouldn't be and lots of people deluding themselves about things that are never going to happen. Dostoevsky is all about the sort of people who are living as clowns yet are adamant that they are not clowns. And *Crime and Punishment*'s hero Raskolnikov is the really great example of the ultimate unresolved conflict. He is not in denial about being a clown. He is in denial about being a pathetic and weak person who can't and won't face up to his responsibilities. He's a warning: if you don't face your demons, you will end up destroying yourself, and maybe even others. Where Eugene Onegin suffers because he is too strong to admit his own weaknesses, Raskolnikov suffers because he overcompensates for his feelings of inadequacy. Decades before anyone had defined the psychological term 'acting out' (displaying outwardly destructive behaviour instead of facing up to your difficult feelings), Raskolnikov was the poster boy for it.

Dostoevsky began work on *Crime and Punishment* in 1865, and the novel is infused with the political questions of the time. Or, rather, the only ones that mattered to Dostoevsky, such as 'Why is everyone becoming such a godless heathen?' Dostoevsky, as well as being an inveterate gambler and an incredibly psychologically complex and contradictory person (which is what I like about him), was a Slavophile and a religious man. He was deeply conservative. The character of Raskolnikov represents a warning about atheism and symbolizes Dostoevsky's fear that Russia is about to be overrun with rationalists and nihilists (who are against God) and utopian socialists (an ideology which he sees as selfish and naive). Raskolnikov's tortured story is a call for Russia to stay true to its roots and to believe in God and the essential goodness of the Slavophile path.

For Dostoevsky, the freedom that Raskolnikov represents is dangerous and egotistical. While you might disagree with almost all Dostoevsky's views above, they are understandable. They are very similar to the views of your average reactionary: 'We don't want things to change, they're fine as they are and anyone who thinks that they have a better way of making life fairer is mad.' I disagree. But I get it.

In the novel, Rodion Romanovich Raskolnikov (both an excellent name and a lovely patronymic) is a former student seeking a path in life. He is good-looking and arrogant. He has delusions of grandeur and dreams of achieving something amazing that will transform the fortunes of his family. His dreams are not selfless, though. What he really wants is to achieve greatness. According to Raskolnikov, boring, normal people 'preserve the world and increase and multiply, where extraordinary people move the world and guide it to its goal'. I cannot help thinking that, if Raskolnikov had had Twitter, he would not have needed to kill anyone. He could have just lived out all his grandiose fantasies on there, tapping and trolling away. Why overcome inner conflict when you can harass other people with annoying hashtags? And it's so much less effort than tracking down moneylenders to kill.

Instead, Raskolnikov has to face up to his problems. Supposedly. His mother and his unmarried sister are living in precarious circumstances. He wants to be a man and 'save' them. It's a letter from his mother that is the catalyst for his crime – or, at least, the excuse. Quite how Dostoevsky achieves the trick of making it seem completely normal that Raskolnikov decides to solve all his problems by killing the old woman moneylender . . . Well, this is the really impressive thing about *Crime and Punishment*.

Because this is indeed the trick the author achieves. Raskolnikov has a sort of 'Napoleon' syndrome, as it is described in the novel. He believes that he is above the normal laws of society and that he is capable of great deeds. He decides to commit the crime to prove it.

Nietzsche was only eleven when Dostoevsky was creating Raskolnikov, but the character embodies many of the philosopher's later ideas about the Übermensch (the man who believes he is above the common herd and not subject to normal ideas of morality). Dostoevsky also uses Raskolnikov to demonstrate how selfish and sick people become when they turn away from God. They begin to believe they can achieve anything and that it's all in their hands; no need to wait for any guidance from God. Weirdly, this is not dissimilar to some of the ideas expressed by the self-actualization movement so popular today. (Not that I'm suggesting self-help books encourage you to kill anyone, but they do encourage you to believe that you are capable of great things, which is not such a long way away from Raskolnikov's position.) I think Dostoevsky would not have enjoyed the current godless vogue for self-help books, and he would have absolutely hated R. Kelly's hit single 'I Believe I Can Fly'. Believing he could touch the sky, believing that he could soar and go running through that open door . . . all that was Raskolnikov's problem. And it does not work out well for him.

Tortured on the one hand by the idea that he might kill the old lady and turn out to feel bad about it (something he hopes won't happen but he nonetheless dreads) and on the other by the idea that he might not be able to kill her and then feel like a failure (something he feels like already and can't bear), Raskolnikov roams the streets of St Petersburg. He ends up at the old lady's house. He kills her, and he also kills her half-sister, who has witnessed the crime. He is in such a state afterwards (not being much of an Übermensch, after all), however, that he only manages to steal a few bits and bobs. So he kills two people for nothing. The rest of the novel is about his path to self-loathing, confession and, finally, redemption.

There's a flaw here for me. It would have been a very different novel if Raskolnikov had 'successfully' murdered the old lady and 'achieved' something, instead of botching the job somewhat. He could have paid off his family's debts, helped his sister avoid marrying a series of lecherous old gits who were queuing up for her and set himself up in life in some way. Of course, at some point, he would start to feel bad. Maybe Dostoevsky was too impatient. He is eager to punish Raskolnikov before he has even committed the crime. As far as Dostoevsky is concerned, Raskolnikov should never have wanted to kill the old lady in the first place. In reality, the novel succeeds because Dostoevsky has more in common with Raskolnikov than he cares to admit. He knows what it is like to be desperate for money. (Dostoevsky died owing money, despite his immense fame and success by that point.) He knows what it is like to feel so angry with someone that you want to kill them (I think he probably would have killed Turgenev, given half a chance). He is too close to Raskolnikov for comfort. So perhaps Dostoevsky was afraid to make Raskolnikov's crime a success, in case it made explicit his own not so secret desire for wealth, revenge and success. (If we are talking self-awareness, Dostoevsky's was buried under many, many layers of self-loathing. No one was more plagued by inner conflict.)

There's a parallel with Tolstoy's relationship to Anna Karenina here, and the trouble with what our subconscious desires. Tolstoy wanted to use Anna consciously to demonstrate an immorality that should be punished. But this plan doesn't entirely work out because the author subconsciously sympathizes with her too much. Similarly, Dostoevsky wants to use Raskolnikov as an example of a despicable human being. And yet Dostoevsky gets right under the character's skin, almost as if he knows what it's like to be inside Raskolnikov's head. Both novels work because they are fiendishly complex, not least because both authors appear to be protesting just a little bit too much. Perhaps more disturbing than Raskolnikov's apparent weirdness is how ordinary he is. Far from being the outsider oddball Dostoevsky might have intended, Raskolnikov is painfully similar to us. He gets tired. He gets frustrated. He gets hungry. He even has some means of controlling his rage: he only has to eat some food to calm his mania. 'One glass of beer and a rusk and my mind grows keen, my thoughts clear, my resolution firm. Bah, how paltry it all is.' He likes having vodka and a pasty and has to have a lie-down afterwards. Poor lamb, he's not murderous, he's just tired and hungry.

Like *Anna Karenina*, *Crime and Punishment* was inspired by a real-life story. Where Tolstoy had Anna of All the Pies, Dostoevsky had Gerasim Chistov. In Moscow in August 1865, Chistov, a merchant's son who belonged to the religious denomination known as the Old Belief, murdered two elderly women while robbing their mistress. The time of day was the same as Raskolnikov's crime, and Chistov also used an axe. Just as Tolstoy borrowed parts of the pie-eater's name for his fictional version, so Dostoevsky converted the word for 'Old Believer' – *raskolnik* – into the surname of his murderer. He started work on the novel later that month.

First and foremost, Dostoevsky intended the book as an attack against nihilism. As the historian Ronald Hingley writes, Dostoevsky had spent a long time brooding on his ideas about the path of Russia. These ideas were not always necessarily very sensible. Hingley is a sympathetic and loving biographer who is very much on the side of his subject. He describes Dostoevsky as 'this neurotic, hypersensitive, habitually over-reacting, never-relaxing man'. If this is what his friends say, I'd hate to hear from his enemies.

Before he decided to become a writer, Dostoevsky had lived a peculiar life. He was from a fairly well-off family descended from Lithuanian nobles. (Ironically, in view of the fact that he would become so obsessed with being Russian. Ah, how I sympathize with that fixation.) His father was a military doctor who struggled to keep up the appearance of being middle class. The family had a country estate but could barely afford to maintain it. The estate had a hundred serfs and his father had a hereditary title. But, still, later in life, Dostoevsky always had a chip on his shoulder about being from a 'lesser' class, compared to Tolstoy and Turgenev. I think it's also safe to assume that his parents didn't always get on that well, as his mother once wrote a letter to his father, assuring her husband that he was the father of her latest child: 'I swear to you that my present pregnancy is the seventh and firmest bond in our love for each other. My love for you is pure, holy, chaste and passionate, and has never swerved since the day of our marriage.' That is a pretty extraordinary thing to write to the man by whom you have already borne six children.

Dostoevsky's father was apparently a colourful character, not much loved by the serfs on his estate. Later, Dostoevsky's daughter was to claim that her grandfather had been murdered by his serfs who had 'smothered him with the cushions of his own carriage'. There are many competing stories like this about his death: that he was 'forcibly choked with vodka'; that he was 'lynched by a dozen peasants'; and that he was 'smothered while his sexual organs were crushed between stones'. (Good grief. A crime for which, surely, there's no sufficient punishment. Ouch.) None of these accounts comes from Dostoevsky himself, who was eighteen at the time of his father's death, but presumably, these are rumours he would have known about. And they already sound like something out of his novels. They make Raskolnikov's bungled axe attack sound kind.

At the age of sixteen, Dostoevsky was sent to the army's Chief Engineering Academy, an experience which he considered to have ruined his life. He was held back a year for 'incompetent drill', fuelling his paranoia and his obsession with the fact that he was doomed to occupy an inferior status compared to others. This became increasingly channelled into a sort of xenophobia. Before he was twenty, he was already known for expressing 'an intense and uncontrollable loathing for non-Russians in general'. Dostoevsky had to plead with his flatmate 'never again to introduce him to foreigners': 'If I don't watch out, they'll marry me to a Frenchwoman, and then it will be goodbye once and for all to Russian literature.' Luckily for Frenchwomen everywhere, Dostoevsky was known for fainting or having a fit every time he met a beautiful woman, so they were at little risk of falling prey to his 'charms'.

He convinced himself, meanwhile, that writing would be his chosen profession. His first novel, *Poor Folk*, was an immediate success, admitting him to St Petersburg's literary circles, where he was hailed as 'a new Gogol'. This was a poisoned chalice for Dostoevsky, though, who at first enjoyed the attention but soon became apt to clash with anyone who argued with him, which was, essentially, everyone. His next novel was *The Double*. This is an extraordinary book about a government clerk called Golyadkin who encounters a man who is his doppelgänger. At first, they become friends, but then the double starts taking over his life. It's clearly a portrait of mental disintegration. It had mixed reviews. And the more Dostoevsky's writings became known, the more he became a subject of ridicule, some of which was fuelled by Turgenev, sowing the seeds of their later feud abroad.

Rude verses appeared, claiming that Dostoevsky was eaten up with envy for Gogol. He quickly established a reputation as a rather freakish character, known for his tics: twitching and tweaking his beard, biting his moustache or swearing. There are various academic discussions about whether this was epilepsy, Tourette's or St Vitus' Dance, and Freud himself later wrote his own casebook on Dostoevsky. He clearly had epileptic seizures and wrote to his brother of suffering 'all kinds of attacks'. Freud decided it was all in the writer's mind, brought on as a reaction to the death of his father.

I love the darkness and the black humour of Dostoevsky's work, but it's almost painful to read if you know anything about the writer's life. Although his fiction is not autobiographical, his mental torment is in every character. I cannot bear to think how much he must have suffered in his strange life. Just as he became known as a writer, he was arrested for political conspiracy. At that time, aged twenty-eight, he faced a mock execution in front of a firing squad at which each of the victims was dressed in a white shroud with long sleeves and a hood. To make matters worse, the man reading out the death sentence had a stutter. At the last minute, the Tsar intervened and Dostoevsky was sent to Siberia for four years instead. And, remember, all this is happening to someone who already suffered from severe epilepsy and was, arguably, mentally unstable or, at the very least, sensitive and fragile.

Dostoevsky meant to show through Raskolnikov that Russia was sick and needed to return to her roots. His early writings about his country give a foretaste of what was to come. After serving four years in the Siberian prison and a fair amount of time in the army (which he hated), he married an irritable woman who could barely tolerate his epilepsy. He later wrote of her, 'She and I were decidedly unhappy together owing to her weird, pernickety and pathologically fantastic character.'

Clearly, this would not put you in a good mood. And already Dostoevsky was a very angry young man. When he first settled in St Petersburg, he wrote some articles for a magazine he co-founded with his brother. They were ultra-nationalist in tone and content. Russians never take offence, as other peoples do, he wrote. Russians can speak all languages. And they never boast, he added. (I can testify that none of these things is true of Russians, or indeed of any nationality. Possibly, they may be true of a species on *Star Trek*. But the bit about never getting offended is especially untrue of Russians. If experience has taught me anything, it's that Russians love to get offended. But good on Dostoevsky for being a patriot, I guess.) There is something sad about Dostoevsky's desperate protestations here, that reminds me of my own crazed insistence that I must force myself to speak poetry like Akhmatova and swear off speaking English for months at a time in order to feel 'more authentically Russian'. These are the insistences of a person who is not facing up to inner conflict. Dostoevsky had Tatar, Lithuanian, Belorussian and Polish blood but considered himself to be 'a Russian of the Russians'. See what I mean about delusional clowns not wanting to be the thing they really are?

All the accounts of Dostoevsky's life feature him doing things that make you think, 'Oh, Fedya, what have you done now?' (Diminutive of Fyodor. Tick.) This is a man who wrote a novel entitled *The Idiot* and yet was constantly, unintentionally, doing idiotic things which caused him harm. He may have loved Russia, but he didn't love many of the Russians he met while in Western Europe. On encountering Herzen, he wrote to a friend: ' . . . our intellectuals. What wretched insignificant scum puffed up with vanity! What shit!' On a visit to London, he is disgusted by the gin, the soot and the prostitutes. He particularly hated Crystal Palace. He left, appalled, for Paris, which he hated even more: 'By God, the French do make me sick.' I think he did derive some joy from his love of women, although positive emotions were evidently difficult for him. After his wedding to his first wife, he suffered epileptic fits for four days. His second wife, Anna Grigorievna Snitkina, was, however, a godsend. She was introduced to him when she became stenographer for his novel *The Gambler*. On their first meeting she described him as 'weird, shattered, battered, exhausted, sick' and wearing a stained jacket. (Hmm. The ideal blind date.) Thanks to her shorthand, the novel was written in twenty-six days. On the day the book was finished, she arrived wearing 'a gown of lilac silk' which he found so charming it made him blush. They married three months later.

But he couldn't stop himself from being Dostoevsky. He had to drink two cups of coffee before anyone could speak to him in the morning. (This was one of his least objectionable habits, admittedly.) His second wife felt that she was forced to dress 'like a woman twice her age' because Dostoevsky got jealous that other men were looking at her. There were constant financial problems, partly because Dostoevsky was supporting other family members and partly because he gambled all the time. Husband and wife argued over the fact that his overcoat was often at the pawn shop, even in winter. They travelled to Europe to avoid Dostoevsky's creditors (and so that he could argue with Turgenev). The accounts from their time abroad of the scale of Dostoevsky's self-defeating behaviour are truly jaw-dropping. He ends up having to pawn the legendary lilac dress at one point, along with his wife's jewellery: 'brooches, earrings, wedding ring, fur coat, shawl'. He declared that their time spent in Europe was, for him, 'worse than Siberia'.

Even Dostoevsky experienced some joy on these trips, though. When he won at gambling, he would buy his wife flowers and fruit and once returned with all her favourite foods: 'caviar, bilberries, French mustard and even the edible fungi known as *ryzhiki* [saffron milk caps]; a Russian delicacy which, she claimed, no other husband in the world would have unearthed in this benighted German spa'.

His time in Europe was overshadowed by a terrible event which happened in Geneva: the death of their baby, Sonya. She died of pneumonia at the age of three months, a year after their wedding. Dostoevsky was inconsolable: 'People try to comfort me by saying I'll have other children. But where is Sonya? Where is the tiny creature? To restore her to life I'd accept the torments of crucifixion.' They went on to have three more children, although their son Alexey suffered from epilepsy like his father and died at the age of three after a two-hour seizure. Nonetheless, family life seemed to bring Dostoevsky some small comfort: he loved buying presents for his children and nursed them when they were ill.

There is a lot of theorizing about Dostoevsky's relationship with women, with some arguing that he harboured an intense hatred for them and subconsciously blamed them for all his ills. He certainly loved his second wife, when he was not pawning her favourite dress, that is. He once wrote in a letter to her when he was taking the waters in Germany that he had had a dream about her 'in a seductive form' which caused 'nocturnal consequences'. If anything, I wonder if Dostoevsky's problem was that he did not let himself enjoy life very much at all and possibly did not experience as many nocturnal consequences as perhaps he could have done. We all need nocturnal consequences in order to manage our internal conflicts, if nothing else.

He adored his mother. He carried a miniature which had been hers, an angel with wings which had the inscription *J'ai le cœur tout plein d'amour/Quand l'aurez-vous à votre tour?* ('I have a heart full of love/When will you feel the same?') As a child, he had had some happy moments. The family had once seen a show with a trapeze artist impersonating 'a Brazilian ape'. (I don't know how they knew the ape was Brazilian. Maybe it was drinking a caipirinha.) Little Fedya came home and 'was an ape for weeks'. (I would have paid a lot to see this.) Certainly, his father was a cruel man, but he found some solace in his mother.

However, Dostoevsky's attitude to women is obvious not so much because of the facts of his biography but because of the female characters in his books. He writes very differently about them compared to Tolstoy. Where Tolstoy sees women as having an internal world and feelings and thoughts similar to those of men, Dostoevsky's female characters only really exist in relation to the men – and all his tormented protagonists are men. In *Crime and Punishment*, Raskolnikov's problems are largely caused by women: he wants to save his mother and sister from shame. He is 'saved' by a woman, his confessor, Sonia Marmeladova. She offers him comfort, even though she knew one of his victims (Lizaveta, the half-sister of the moneylender). Sonia has been described as a character who only really exists in the role of a 'therapist' for Raskolnikov, giving him a chance to tell his story and express his remorse. Dostoevsky is not great at offering remedies in his work, but this is one he comes up with time and time again: speaking to a confessor figure (often a woman) is one way to ease your inner torment. If only he had lived in the age of 'Dear Deirdre', he might have been happier.

While Tolstoy is interested in using the individual as a way of expressing universal experience, Dostoevsky is far more self-absorbed. This isn't necessarily a bad thing. It's helpful to look at both approaches to life: epic sweep versus extreme introspection. There's an idea that you are either a Tolstoy person or a Dostoevsky person. I once met the Russian novelist Boris Akunin, who writes Sherlock Holmes-style mysteries about a nineteenth-century Russian detective. The first question he asked me was this: 'Are you Tolstoy party or Dostoevsky party?' I wasn't sure how to answer this, as I love both, for different reasons, but I was worried this would make me look like an indecisive person. I said, 'Dostoevsky party', adding rather lamely, 'Although I'm up for any party, really.' He was Tolstoy party.

Isaiah Berlin posed a version of this question in his essay *The Hedgehog and the Fox*. It became a question everyone wanted to pose about themselves, 'Am I a hedgehog or a fox?' Berlin did not mean it to be taken so seriously. But people love classifications and wanted to work out which group they belonged to. Dostoevsky is a hedgehog, a person who defines the world through a single idea or has one, big message. (No one, including Berlin, has quite seemed able to define exactly what that message is for Dostoevsky, but I suspect it is something like 'Believe in God (and Russia) or you will die, heathen.') 'The fox knows many things, but the hedgehog knows one big thing,' wrote Berlin, quoting the ancient Greek poet Archilochus. The fox, however, accepts that life has many confusing aspects and many pluralities. There can't be a unifying principle; life is too diverse. Berlin concludes, fascinatingly, that Tolstoy was tormented towards the end of his life because he desperately wanted to be a hedgehog but he was at heart a fox. His religious convictions said 'hedgehog'; his instinct said 'fox'. He killed off the fox because it went against his religious convictions. Poor fox. I'm going to start weeping now. (I don't know what the clown-who-wasn't-a-clown would have made of all this, by the way. I suspect he would have been Team Hedgehog all the way, regardless of the philosophical implications.)

What does all this mean? I think it's about how comfortable you are with accepting contradictions in yourself and in the world. It's about whether you can see beyond your own internal conflicts to a world outside yourself. If you can accept, or at least examine, those things, you are a fox. If you can't accept them and you want to believe in that one big thing ('We must serve God,' for example), you are a hedgehog. According to Berlin's analysis, hedgehogs are doomed to suffer more than foxes because they want everything (and everyone) to fit into a pattern. This tallies with Dostoevsky's obsession with the idea that Russia must follow a particular path, and it's the path he has decided upon. Tolstoy looks at the path Russia is following and examines it in detail. In the final analysis, I think it's the difference between being judgemental and being open-minded. It's the difference between being able to live with some measure of inner conflict and being unable to tolerate any inner conflict and instead gambling and twitching loads and ending up pawning your wife's favourite lilac dress.

This seems like an easy choice. Obviously, being open-minded is going to make you a happier person than being a judgemental one is. But it's not as straightforward as it seems. Believing in one unifying principle (hedgehog) instead of living with the possibility of uncertainty and contradiction (fox) is very attractive. Tolstoy tried to be like Dostoevsky and be a hedgehog. He tried to judge everything, including himself, to improve constantly and conform to a unifying system (and a judgemental God). But it didn't make him happy because he was at heart a pluralist who believed – as he showed in *Anna Karenina* and *War and Peace* – that it takes many people with different ideas to make up a world. The fox is (strangely for a real-life fox) empathetic and aware that other people have thoughts and feelings, too. The hedgehog thinks, 'Why doesn't everyone think like me?'

Crime and Punishment is feverishly dark and entertaining, but there is also something profoundly sad about it. It's perhaps because, as Berlin suggests, a hedgehog like Dostoevsky can never quite convince us that things are as simple as he'd like to make out. Raskolnikov is not pure evil. Possibly, he's not evil at all, he's just demented. We sympathize with him. We are not supposed to identify with Raskolnikov, and yet we do: 'You come to a certain limit and if you do not overstep it, you will be unhappy, but if you do overstep it, perhaps you will be even more unhappy.' This is true of Raskolnikov's crime. He feels he must do it in order to be complete, even if he knows he will be damned. And if he doesn't do it, he will not be saved either because he will still be unhappy. Many things in life feel like this, not just a decision as to whether to murder an old lady moneylender. We love Raskolnikov even though he is a murderer because we identity with his suffering.

There's a quote from a letter Dostoevsky wrote in 1879 that sums up the sadness of this vision: 'Life is such a ridiculous business – sublime only in its inner significance.' Yes, on occasion that's true. But life only really has meaning when we turn away from 'inner significance' and look at ourselves in the context of other people. While Dostoevsky has profound, sometimes disturbing, insight into the human mind, Tolstoy has empathy for the human condition. The trick for us as readers is to combine the two, something neither writer, both tortured in different ways, managed to do in his lifetime.

When I was immersed in my own little Russian world, I was too self-absorbed to see that I was getting just as lost as Raskolnikov. Acute, hedgehog-style self-absorption is not pretty, and it's not healthy for anyone. During that year in St Petersburg, I had convinced myself that my destiny was to be Russian, to marry my Ukrainian boyfriend and to embrace the destiny that my name suggested. Over the course of that year, I went native. On the plus side, my Russian was great. On the negative side, I had become a different person. There were times when I barely recognized myself. I was weighed down by inner conflict. Not that I could see that at the time.

On one occasion, I was taking the tram home from a lesson where I had been teaching English. Usually, I didn't take the tram, because the wait was too long and I got impatient and I preferred to walk. On this day, I was tired, so had decided to accept the wait. When the tram eventually arrived, I sat opposite a middle-aged woman who looked pale and sickly. She seemed agitated. The tram was fairly empty, but there were at least another dozen people seated near us, and I monitored their faces to see if they had noticed the woman. They had. But no one did anything. We all waited to see what would happen. When we were waiting at a red light, she began convulsing uncontrollably and foaming at the mouth. Time stopped. I had been told not to make it obvious to anyone that I was a foreigner; otherwise, I would cause trouble for myself or for them. This was a time when there were still fairly few foreigners about and you did your best to go around unnoticed. It was too big a test of my Russian for me to risk doing anything. And, in any case, what could I do to help this woman? She kept on shaking and dribbling. Her eyes fell backwards in her head, the whites of them raised up. All this lasted a matter of seconds, but it seemed like hours. The lights changed and the tram lunged forward. Two men got up to help her, alerted the driver and dragged her off the tram. I had sat there, having said and done nothing. I'm pretty sure she died. I got off at the next stop and forgot all about it.

I had gone native. No, I was worse than native. I had become so preoccupied with my internal conflict about appearing to be Russian at all times and in all places that I no longer knew who I was at all. I had lost my identity and I had lost my humanity. I wasn't just a hedgehog with one big idea. Or a clown pretending to be something other than a clown. I had gone full-on porcupine. And I was stuck inside the tunnel.

7. How to Live with the Feeling That the Grass is Always Greener: *Three Sisters* by Anton Chekhov

(Or: Don't keep going on about Moscow)

'Oh my God, I dream of Moscow every night.
I'm just like a lunatic.'

I have often felt that what I suffer most from in life is the sense that the grass is always greener on the other side. This is a combination of two things: first, the feeling that everyone else has got it better than me (yes, I know, boo hoo, let me get out the world's tiniest violin), and, second, the idea that if only I were somewhere else, everything would be fine (yes, I know this is foolish, but I'm just being honest). The danger of this way of thinking is summed up by two cautionary Russian proverbs: 'If you chase two rabbits, you will not catch either one' and 'As long as the sun shines, one does not ask for the moon.' Or as my grandmother said the time I wanted a third jam tart (there were three flavours and I hadn't tried lemon curd yet), 'Don't be greedy.'

We all know the feeling that everyone else is having a better time than us. It's 'if only' syndrome. If only you were somewhere else instead of being where you are. If only you had got that job instead of it being given to that woman you hate. If only you could be in two places at once. We even think this way when we're happy. 'Things are good but . . . wouldn't it be nice to be on the balcony of a flat in Paris with a view of the Sacré-Cœur?' Or, as they say in Russian, 'Life is better there where we are not.' This, said in an extremely categorical and depressing voice, is probably the best Russian saying of all time. Is there any more fatalistic thought in human existence?

The problem is, no matter how good we have it, the grass genuinely does seem greener elsewhere. Nowhere is this better illustrated than in Chekhov's play *Three Sisters*, where all the three sisters really want in life is to get back to Moscow, scene of their childhood. Moscow represents a reaction against their present life – which they don't want – and a promise of something better. They want Moscow, Moscow, Moscow. They say it enough times. But what they also want, crucially, is to be somewhere else other than where they are right now. Sound familiar?

It's human nature to think this way and it has no doubt always been thus. But it's perhaps legitimate to argue that, in the modern era, this feeling can become so acute it's almost unbearable. After all, up until about a hundred years ago, we all had fairly predetermined roles in life. Your fortunes might wax and wane, but you were more or less confined to the circumstances you were born in, whether you liked it or not. You could pine for some other kind of life but you had no real chance of achieving it. Also, back then, you were not constantly assailed by images and information about other people's lives elsewhere. In today's world, the three sisters could have indulged themselves by following any one of 26 million hashtags on Instagram extolling the joys of Muscovite life in glorious Technicolor, and regularly updated. Who knows, maybe this would have scratched the itch and made them want to go to Moscow less. Or maybe it would have made them all the more mad for Moscow.

Chekhov's brilliance lies in capturing something important about a life change that was happening at the time he was writing: people were starting to be able to affect their own lives, change their class, break out of the confines of their gender. I like to think it's significant that it's *Three Sisters* and not 'Three Brothers'. If it were 'Three Brothers', the brothers could just go and live in Moscow and it would be a very short play, set largely in Moscow. (Even by Chekhov's time, men still had far more ability to change their life circumstances than women.) Nowadays, we have different feelings about wanting to be somewhere we're not. Of course, envy and regret are natural emotions, after all, and there has never been a historical era where everyone can have everything they want. But in modern times, we also think this way because we know the truth: our own life decisions played at least some role in bringing us to where we are. We have a choice. If we want to be in Moscow and we're not – well, we have only ourselves to blame.

This wasn't true of the sisters in Chekhov's play. They did not have so much agency over their lives. But they had more agency than women of a previous generation, and perhaps that responsibility weighed heavily on them. In *Three Sisters*, Irina, Masha and Olga want nothing more than to go to Moscow. Or, at least, to be fair, Irina (the youngest) and Olga (the eldest) both express a wish to go to Moscow. Olga wants to recapture past glories. Irina wants to seize a new future. Masha doesn't care as much about Moscow. She just wants to get away from her nightmare Latin-quoting husband and to have a fling with Vershinin, the army officer married to a suicidal and temperamental wife.

It's never clear in the play precisely where they are geographically. We know they must be somewhere in a provincial town not that far from Moscow. Chekhov doesn't need to make it clear exactly where they are because it's obvious enough that it's 'the provinces'. But I also wonder if it's intentional. It doesn't matter where they are. It matters where they aren't. The answer to where they are is: 'Not Moscow. Which is where we want to be. Not Moscow. And if we're not there, who cares where we are?' Chekhov knows that we are better at defining ourselves by what we lack than by what we have. There's a rather pathetic passive aggression to this. But Chekhov takes it seriously and sympathizes with it, while also realizing how ridiculous it makes us. We will never get to Moscow. And we will never see the good around us in the place where we are.

In the first big speech of the play, it's Olga who sets up Moscow as the ultimate destination. 'I remember perfectly that it was early in May and that everything in Moscow was flowering then . . .' Her passion for Moscow is strange, in a way. She's twenty-eight years old (age is specified in the cast list, just like in Turgenev), she left Moscow at the age of seventeen and yet she still calls it 'home'. It's easy to see that it's not really Moscow she wants. What she really wants is to be seventeen and full of potential, with her whole life ahead of her. Not to be nearly thirty and, as she would see it, on the shelf.

Irina's affinity for Moscow is even stranger. She would have been eight or nine years old when they left. Why should she care about Moscow? And yet she has inherited Olga's negativity and has observed Masha's disillusioned marriage close up. Plus, the sisters' brother, Andrey, who has an annoying wife, is extremely dull and has failed to reach his full potential: 'The summit of my ambitions is to become a member of the council . . . I, who dream every night that I'm a professor of Moscow University, a famous scholar of whom all Russia is proud.' The cry of 'To Moscow, Moscow, Moscow' is just code for 'Please don't say this is my life. There must be something better somewhere else. Surely?' And also: 'Please someone get me away from the nightmarish people who appear to be my friends and family.' We get it. The grass is always greener.

Three Sisters is often seen as a work about isolation, both literal and metaphorical. The sisters feel they're isolated because of where they are. But they are also emotionally isolated from each other because they judge their siblings' choices and attitudes. The 'other' place everyone wants to be is portrayed as somewhere you never feel judged, you never feel sad, you never feel lonely, everyone loves you and you achieve exactly what you dreamed of. Who would not want the address of this place? This is one timeshare I would sign up for immediately. (I don't think I could live there permanently. You have to be able to be a bit neurotic from time to time, otherwise you'd go mad. Who really wants to get everything they've ever asked for?)

On and on it goes, the obsession with Moscow. Andrey: 'In Moscow you can sit in an enormous restaurant where you don't know anybody and where nobody knows you and you don't feel all the same that you're a stranger. And here you know everybody and everybody knows you, and you're a stranger. A lonely stranger.' Real life – what's right here – is so disappointing. But what's over there . . . it's so much more satisfying. Irina: 'What I wanted, what I hoped to get, just that is lacking here. Oh my God, I dream of Moscow every night. I'm just like a lunatic.' Ferapont, the elderly peasant, knows the truth, of course. Moscow, he says, is a place where people eat forty or fifty pancakes in a sitting and die from it. (I would really like to go to this place.)

What everyone lacks in this play is a sense of purpose. While several peasants dance attendance on them, bringing them things and complaining about competitive overeating of pancakes, they moan about being drowsy and tired and drained of meaning, drawling on idly about how wonderful it must be to be a 'workman': 'How fine it is to be a workman . . . who breaks stones in the street, or a shepherd, or a schoolmaster . . . or an engine-driver . . . It's better to be an ox or just a horse . . . than a young woman who wakes up at twelve o'clock, has her coffee in bed and spends two hours dressing. Oh it's awful!' Chekhov makes it clear from the comedy of this that his heart bleeds.

Vershinin is the voice of the author in this play. He's the one who knows that happiness is always something on the horizon. We need to head towards it, but, once we get there, it moves away again. So Moscow is not the solution. Just in the same way as the prisoner mentioned by Vershinin sees birds in the sky only when he is locked up and stops noticing them once he is free again, uprooting ourselves in search of a dream is not the answer. 'When you go to live in Moscow, you'll not notice it, in just the same way. There can be no happiness for us. It only exists in our wishes.' (Vershinin is not immune to Chekhov's black humour either, though. Shortly after this sensible, philosophical speech, he says, 'My wife has poisoned herself again. I must go. I'll go out quietly.' I love the almost-Britishness of this. 'Oh, how jolly inconvenient, someone has tried to commit suicide again. Please do excuse me.')

One of the most darkly amusing moments in *Three Sisters* is in Act 3, when there is a huge, dangerous blaze, causing a massive fire alarm to go off. Lives are in danger here, and what do they talk about? The fact that once there was a fire in Moscow. Of course! Still, the fire does act as a wake-up call; reality starts to set in with Irina: 'We'll never go away to Moscow . . . I see that we'll never go . . .' Although, moments later, she is imploring Olga to take them there.

The significance of Moscow is not only that it represents a better life; it represents a shared dream. Delusion works only if others share it with us. The three sisters have to back each other up. None of them stands up and says, 'Oh, come on, stop being ridiculous. The whole Moscow thing is never going to happen.' The delusion is something that binds them all together and gives them a common sense of purpose. In this sense, Moscow is not necessarily a bad thing. It represents the hope they all share that things could and might be different. In terms of life lessons, this is a useful one: whatever your delusion about what you need in order to be happy is ('I need to go to Moscow!' 'I need a pay rise!' 'I must buy more shoes!'), it becomes more powerful when it is reinforced by other people.

By Act 4 – the only act in which Moscow is not mentioned – things have soured. We never quite know whether Moscow stands for hope or for delusion. But whichever is the case, 'Moscow' as an idea has disappeared by the end of the play. The final disaster is not so much for Olga but for Irina. 'I am already twenty-three. I have already been at work for a long while and my brain has dried up. And I've grown thinner and plainer, older and there is no relief of any sort. I'm in despair and I can't understand how it is that I am still alive, that I haven't killed myself.' Cheer up, Irina!

There are some little clues strewn through *Three Sisters* which seem to me an indication that perhaps the 'awful', non-Moscow place where we find ourselves is never quite so bad as we think it is. Chekhov likes to mention food and drink, and they seem to have some great stuff on offer right where they are: goose baked with cabbage, Caucasian onion soup, *chehartma* (a Georgian soup), champagne. Do you really need to go to Moscow when you have all these things on your doorstep? Chekhov is, above all, a comedic dramatist, and you can't help thinking that he's really trying to flag up that the sisters' pining for Moscow is something of a First World problem. (I would have also listed *kvass*, as Chekhov does, but it's pretty disgusting, so I didn't. It is a fermented beverage made from rye bread which tastes exactly as you would expect a fermented beverage made from rye bread to taste. It should not be listed in the same context as champagne.)

Nabokov once described the tone of Chekhov's stories as evoking a colour that was 'between the colour of an old fence and that of a low cloud'. This doesn't sound like much of a compliment. And yet it's a good description of what Chekhov does. If Dostoevsky is the deep red of blood on an axe, Chekhov is the colour of sudsy dishwater. But in a good way. Chekhov deals in suggestion. He evokes. He doesn't preach. And he isn't afraid of small, domestic settings. He doesn't look for the grand plan or the sweep of history. If Tolstoy is like someone creating an opera on the page, Chekhov is finishing a rather tricky jigsaw puzzle.

Virginia Woolf argued that there was a certain precision about life that you only get from Chekhov. She wrote about the experience of reading in translation and of how a reader feels when they are connecting to a text written in another language. Why do we fool ourselves that we could hope to grasp any of the meaning when we don't necessarily share the same values? Reading an author who hasn't written in your own language deprives a text of the 'ease' and 'absence of self-consciousness' that Woolf sees as crucial for understanding. Woolf described the Russian writers as being like men stripped of their clothes, manners and personalities after some terrible catastrophe such as an earthquake or a railway accident. This is the state they reach us in when we read them in translation. Why do we even pretend to understand them?

But Chekhov, she said, transcends all this. His way of approaching things, she argued, is so unusual and so blunt that, at first, you feel taken aback and confused: 'What is the point of it, and why does he make a story out of this?' Sometimes, the writing makes no sense and has no particular beginning, middle or end. It often finishes ambiguously or inconclusively. 'Men are at the same time villains and saints. We love and we hate at the same time.' But this, she says, is proper honesty about what life is really like. The grass is not greener on the other side. It's just as bad and just as good as where we already are.

There is something about Chekhov that cuts through to the heart of things: simple, straightforward, human. It's no accident that he was a doctor. Long before he became one of the greatest short-story writers and playwrights of all time, he trained at medical school. He wasn't from a wealthy family to start off with. And by the time he was nearing the age when he wanted to train as a doctor, his father lost a huge amount of money, effectively making Anton Pavlovich the breadwinner. (Quick test. What was his father's name? Yes, that's right. Pavel. I have not mentioned patronymics in a while.) One of the things Chekhov did to make money during this period was to breed and sell goldfinches. Another was to write sketches for newspapers. The more successful he was as a writer, the more his medical career crossed over into his work: by the end of his lifetime, he had portrayed over a hundred doctors as fictional characters.

Whether in spite of or because of his medical training, Chekhov was an optimist. Of all the writers I've mentioned so far, most of them had their moments of being extraordinarily depressed and sometimes even nihilistic. Chekhov is, by contrast, a breath of fresh air. He had no particular reason to be. His upbringing was fairly miserable; he had a bullying father. Chekhov complained that he 'had no childhood in his childhood', even though there were good times, including catching those goldfinches in 'the big, wild garden'.

Chekhov's father was not a nice man, although he perhaps made up for that by being quite a character. He ran a corner store which sold household goods. He used to make his own mustard, and loved caviar. According to one family story, a drowned rat was once discovered in a barrel of cooking oil he wanted to sell. He had the barrel blessed by a priest and sold it anyway. One account of Chekhov's childhood has his brother Nikolai tell how the four brothers shared a feather bed in the room next to the kitchen, constantly breathing in the stink of burnt sunflower oil.

Before the age of five, Chekhov wrote, his first thought on waking was usually, 'Am I going to get beaten today?' And he complained that, after the beating, he was forced to kiss the hand that had punished him. 'When I recall my infancy now, it seems to be hideous,' he wrote in a letter in 1892, referring not so much to the beatings as to the fact that his parents were very keen to attend church and make him sing in the choir. He became an atheist as soon as he possibly could.

Somehow, he rose above it all and became a person of

extraordinary qualities, interested in writing and drama from an early age. At the age of thirteen, he used to paste on a beard and wear fake glasses to get into the theatre. He made his own family theatre, in which he played the mayor in Gogol's *The Government Inspector*, wearing three pillows up his jumper as part of his costume. (This isn't quite as exciting as Dostoevsky impersonating a Brazilian ape for weeks on end, but I still like it.)

Chekhov has the most empathy of all the Russian writers. It could also be said that he led the least writerly life, continuing his medical work, often treating the poor for free. Maybe it's an awful thing to say, but it makes me incredibly sad that Chekhov, a generous, giving and cheery soul, usually with fairly positive insights into the human condition, lived only until the age of forty-four (having by that time suffered from tuberculosis for years), whereas Tolstoy, who could be extremely mean and depressing, lived to twice that age, and used the second half of his life to develop a fairly bleak view of human existence. Them's the breaks. If you believe in fate and look at Chekhov's life, then you'd have to assume that Tolstoy was right in the end: life is arbitrary and awful, and good people die for no reason and bad people get to live long lives for no reason. There's no *Calendar of Wisdom* that can explain that.

Of all the people who would have the right to be resentful about his lot in life and envy that of others, Chekhov was a prime candidate. One night in March 1897, he started haemorrhaging from his mouth while having dinner with his editor and best friend, Suvorin, at the Hermitage restaurant in St Petersburg. His tuberculosis swiftly worsened. Instead of complaining and being bitter, he continued writing, creating some of his most lasting work. He was thirty-seven and so had seven years left to live, and during this time he wrote *Uncle Vanya*, *Three Sisters* and *The Cherry Orchard*, all while suffering pretty horribly. Around the same time, he gave up practising medicine, except on himself, which made him sad, as he had enjoyed being a doctor very much. His own medical treatment shortly after this crisis? 'Creosote vapour inhalation' and 'the application of a poultice'. Soon afterwards, he undertook a '*kumiss* cure'. (*Kumiss* is a beverage made from fermented milk. There is an unfortunate milky pattern emerging here for the terminally ill Russian writers. Also, stop fermenting things, guys! It's gross!) The year after his diagnosis, Chekhov bought land near Yalta and started to spend more time in the Crimea for the sake of his health. The climate was considered to be better for him there. But he wasn't especially happy: 'My life is incomplete. I don't drink, although I like drinking. I like it when it is noisy, but I don't hear any noise. In a word, I now endure the condition of a transplanted tree which hesitates between taking root and starting to wither away,' he wrote in a letter from the Crimea in 1900.

He wrote to Tolstoy often, and the two of them met several times. Chekhov loved Tolstoy's work, but he did not respect his pious message. (See? The 'pious message' thing is Tolstoy trying to turn himself into a hedgehog. Chekhov is definitely a fox. He accepts everything and loves plurality. Also, he did look a bit like a fox.) In return, Tolstoy liked Chekhov as a person, although he thought he wasn't sufficiently opinionated. They first met when Chekhov went to visit Tolstoy at his estate and found the older author submerged while bathing in a pond, his beard floating on the surface. They chatted as Tolstoy bobbed around. Later, Tolstoy praised Chekhov's 'sincerity' and acknowledged that he had discovered new forms of writing. In the few pictures of them together, they look an unlikely pair, Chekhov in a badly fitting dark suit, clipped beard and horn-rimmed glasses, Tolstoy in knee-high riding boots, peasant's smock and something that looks like a white cowboy hat. In one picture, Chekhov's body language is contrite, and Tolstoy is gesturing with his fist and looking directly at him while

Chekhov gazes down at the floor like a schoolboy. Tolstoy was supposed to be the closest to godliness. But it's Chekhov who looks suspiciously like a saint.

One time when Tolstoy was saying goodbye to Chekhov, he whispered in his ear: 'You know, I hate your plays. Shakespeare was a bad writer, and I consider your plays even worse than his.' Chekhov did not take this too badly but said that he felt 'funny and angry' when he thought of this comment about his life's work and reported that Tolstoy had added: 'Where can I follow your character? To the couch in the living room and back. Because your character has no other place to go.'

The story from Chekhov's deathbed is legendary. The doctor wanted to send for oxygen, but Chekhov realized he would be dead by the time it got there. He wanted a glass of champagne instead. 'I haven't had champagne in a long time.' He drank it slowly, stretched out on one side and quietly died. His wife, Olga Knipper, was with him at the time. According to an account inspired by her, 'a huge black moth . . . burst into the room like a whirlwind, beat tormentedly against the burning electric lamps and flew confusedly around the room'. Later the same night, the champagne cork flew out of the unfinished bottle with a bang. I don't really care whether these details are fanciful or not. (It has been suggested that they are.) I want them to be true because they sound like something out of a Chekhov play.

Chekhov was a stoic. In another age, he might have gone towards Zen Buddhism. He clearly learned to live with and accept his own frustrations and difficulties; he didn't want to be someone else or be somewhere else. More things to love about Chekhov? He was a romantic without being sentimental. When he married Olga Knipper, he wrote about how strange a wedding day can feel and the sensation of 'the champagne that you must hold in your hand while you smile vaguely'. He once wrote to her in a letter when they were apart: 'Moscow! Moscow!

These words are not the refrain of *Three Sisters* but of One Husband!' He was said to have a 'gloomy, sad voice'. When he talked about getting older, he said it made him feel like there was 'a jug of sour milk' in his heart. Most of all, he comes across as someone who was extremely kind to other people. Asked to write a short biography of his life, he notes: 'In 1892 I took part in an orgy in the company of V. A. Tihonov at a name-day party.' By this, he means, I think, that they had a few drinks. In a letter written after this party, he tells his friend: 'You are mistaken in thinking you were drunk at Shtcheglov's name-day party. You had had a drop, that was all. You danced when they all danced, and your *jigitivka* on the cabman's box excited nothing but general delight. As for your criticism, it was most likely far from severe, as I don't remember it. I only remember that Vvedensky and I for some reason roared with laughter as we listened to you.' This is the definition of a good person: he makes someone else feel that it was fine for them to be very drunk.

Chekhov is the definition of the sort of empathy Tolstoy began, when he was older, to regret displaying in his work. Chekhov is the master of compassion towards the self and towards others. He is the foxiest of them all. But he also understands the suffering of the hedgehogs and why they think their 'one thing' will save them. The three sisters are all hedgehogs; their one defining ideal is Moscow. The way of the hedgehog is, after all, very persuasive because it is the way of certainty. It's hard to live with the open-ended ways of the fox because it means living with uncertainty. But, ultimately, if you are going to stay sane, you need to be more like Chekhov. It's a lesson I have been very, very slow to learn.

8. How to Keep Going When Things Go Wrong: *One Day in the Life of Ivan Denisovich* by Alexander Solzhenitsyn

(Or: Don't forget to take your spoon to prison with you)

'One must never stop praying. If you have real faith you tell a mountain to move and it will move . . .'

There's a line in *One Day in the Life of Ivan Denisovich* that sounds odd but is instantly graspable: 'Don't open your belly to what doesn't belong to you.' In the context of the book, it's about leaving another prisoner's food package alone. It's about not coveting things that you can't have. It's a warning about wishing too hard to go to Moscow. It relates back to the supposed non-clown who was an animal trainer but still looked like a clown. Don't be delusional about who you are. And it relates back to the massive hedgehog I myself had become. Don't become so fixed on one idea that you lose sight of reality.

During that obsessive year in Russia, I had tried so hard to be someone different that I had become a stranger to myself. (Can I get away with saying that I had become a bit prickly, keen on eating berries and snuffling around in the undergrowth of the Russian language? Hmm.) Everyone else could see it, I expect, in the same way that they could see the clown was wearing a clown costume and therefore couldn't be anything other than a clown. Deep inside, I knew I wasn't really Russian and couldn't stay there for ever and marry my Ukrainian boyfriend who didn't even really like me all that much. I just wanted so desperately to escape and to live up to the promise of my name and to feel like I authentically belonged somewhere. I had a few drama-queen weeks of telling myself that I wouldn't complete my university degree and that I would stay in Russia. But I knew it was all hollow. I said my goodbyes, went home and got on with my life.

Over the next few years, I started a career as a writer in London and travelled frequently to Russia. God's Gift, Son of God's Gift, drifted into the background. I eventually got a job as a contributing editor for a Russian magazine, which meant I could go to Moscow as often as I liked. I met my husband, who turned out to be not from any Russian-speaking country but instead an Englishman from a place forty-two miles away from where I grew up. A not-so-secret part of me still thought I was a bit Russian, and even after I had settled down and was pregnant with my first child, I took a Master's degree, as if to prove it. It was like I had given up but I wanted to show that I hadn't quite given up. For a while, I felt I had resolved the conundrum set in *Three Sisters*: I had the best of both worlds. I didn't have to choose after all.

When the email arrived that revealed the truth about where I was from, I had stopped thinking about my name for a long time. I didn't need to think about it, as I'd come to believe the truth in my own mind. I had always ignored the fact that no one I ever met in Russia recognized the name Groskop and instead focused on the fact that people loved to say that I looked and sounded as if I had a Russian soul. I didn't go around telling people I was Russian. But I didn't need to. Everything about the way I had set up my life made it seem as if I was at least a bit Russian.

Then, when I was in my late twenties, my father received a message from a relative we didn't know about, a cousin in Canada. It was extremely rare for us to receive any kind of correspondence or news from anyone with the name Groskop. We were the only Groskops. The only other ones of us left were

Groscops, which, as discussed, was really not the same thing at all. But here was another Groskop. We knew nothing about him. But he seemed to know an awful lot about us.

I now can't remember exactly when this email arrived, but it must have been at some point in the late 1990s, maybe a bit after that. My grandfather died in the spring of 2001, so it must have been at some point shortly before that. This cousin had traced our family tree back and sent over several documents which, in scratchy fountain pen ink, showed all my grandfather's relatives, mostly people we knew about. It all looked familiar and genuine. Here were uncles and brothers and all kinds of names my grandad recognized but had not thought about in years. He knew all these people. There were a few names that were new to most of us in the family, but my grandad could immediately place them and say who they were. My grandmother, even though she wasn't born into our family but had married into it, also recognized these 'new' names and started telling stories about people she had met fleetingly in the 1940s. It was definitely our family tree, there was no question about it.

This cousin traced the family tree back to my great-great-grandfather. His name was Gershon, and he had come to Stockton-on-Tees in 1861. It listed all his children and their descendants, right down to my generation. All the names and places were correct. They'd started out in Stockton as market traders, then many of the men went on to work as boilermakers. As the work dried up, a contingent of Groskops moved to Barry Island in Wales, again to work as boilermakers. It all made sense: my grandad was born in Barry. Finally, these documents listed the birthplace of Gershon, the place he had left: Łódź, Poland. So, he was Polish. And, judging by all the names, clearly, we were Jewish. I had been in the ballpark. But I had been in the wrong ballpark, or at least several hundred miles out. I had learned the wrong language and absorbed the wrong identity. I wasn't Russian. I was just someone who had opened their belly to what didn't belong to them. It didn't feel good.

The 'belly' scene in *One Day in the Life of Ivan Denisovich* comes towards the end of the book. It's near the end of the day. The inmates of a Soviet prison camp are about to be counted before being sent to their barracks for the night. Ivan Denisovich has had an eventful day, full of the minor setbacks and small personal triumphs that make up camp life. That night, it becomes obvious that Tsezar, one of the other men in Ivan Denisovich's barracks, has received a parcel. Inmates were, theoretically, allowed to receive these from time to time, although actually taking possession of them was another matter. You might have to bribe one guard with cigarettes to let you collect it, and another to let you take it up to your bunk. Once you had your parcel, you would be swamped with requests for barter and exchange. If no one stole any of the contents, then it was a lucky day indeed.

In this scene, Tsezar's parcel is full of all the things everyone – including Ivan Denisovich – most wants and is rarely allowed to have: 'sausage, condensed milk, a plump smoked fish, pork-fat, rusks, biscuits, two kilogrammes of lump sugar and what looked like butter, as well as cigarettes and pipe tobacco'. Ivan Denisovich doesn't have to see the contents of the package to know what's in it. He knows in one sniff what he's missing.

For Solzhenitsyn, this immediately becomes a moment to demonstrate how important self-denial is, and not just because of an ascetic desire to be better than everyone else in the camp and resist temptation. (Although Solzhenitsyn was all about being an ascetic. Seriously, he was virtually like a character out of the Bible. He even looked like God.) No, resisting temptation is not about displaying your self-control. Rather, it's an opportunity to display your humanity. Be patient. Wait your turn. Be gracious about others having more than you. This is the behaviour that will, ultimately, make you a better person. Your humanity is your identity. Don't try to be something you're not. Solzhenitsyn doesn't say any of this. But it's all there in Ivan Denisovich's reaction. He asks for nothing, he expects nothing. He notices that Tsezar looks drunk on the acquisition of all these marvellous worldly goods. But he, Ivan Denisovich, is able to walk away feeling grateful that Tsezar has given him a spare crust of bread. 'Don't open your belly to what doesn't belong to you.'

The mention of 'belly' − representing hunger, desire and instinct, all the things which make us human but which you are supposed to suppress in prison − is not coincidental. Many of Ivan Denisovich's thoughts are about food and whether he will get more or less to eat on any particular day. At the end of this day, he notes it's been a good one because he got some extra porridge (*kasha*). And then there's his spoon, which he eats with. Ivan Denisovich's spoon is his pride and joy. It represents personal freedom and the joy of individuality. He has something no one else has: he has his own spoon. He must hide it, of course, because no one must know that you've kept a scrap of individuality about your person. He keeps it in his *valenki*, his boots. It represents his dignity and the part of him that no one can touch. He calls it his 'baby'. That spoon gives him hope. As long as he is not licking plates but is using his spoon, he is still a human being. The way to keep going in the worst of circumstances? Hold on to who you really are.

One other memorable aspect of *One Day in the Life of Ivan Denisovich* is the way Solzhenitsyn writes about smell and the nose. It's not just the scents that he evokes, although he does this a lot. Obviously, it doesn't take very much imagination to understand what it must be like to be in prison, where you're not allowed the basic small joys of life, like the smell of a freshly baked loaf or newly mown grass, everyday olfactory experiences that − yes, again − make us human without even realizing it.

Every single smell is heightened and Ivan Denisovich's nose is sensitive to every single nuance. But it's not just about sense of smell. It's also about being led – literally – by your nose. There's barely any peripheral vision. It's all about looking down. This works two ways. First, it shows the limited perspective of Ivan Denisovich's world, but, second, it indicates a means of escape. Another way to keep going in the face of disappointment? Sniff out the truth. Sniff out the direction in which hope lies.

Published in 1962, *One Day in the Life of Ivan Denisovich* was the only work by Solzhenitsyn to appear in the USSR during the Soviet period. The 95,000 copies printed sold out instantly and began changing hands on the black market for an extortionate-at-the-time $10 a copy. Everything else he wrote (*Cancer Ward, August 1914, The Gulag Archipelago*) came out in the West, culminating in his Nobel Prize in 1970, which he decided not to go to Stockholm to collect, in case he was not allowed back into Russia. As it was, he got expelled in 1974, when the Soviets had had enough of him.

When *One Day in the Life of Ivan Denisovich* was first reviewed in *The New York Times* in 1964 ('short, sparsely told, eloquent, explosive . . . It took Premier Khrushchev's personal okay to get the story published'), Solzhenitsyn was described as 'a forty-four-year-old mathematics teacher in the old Russian town of Ryazan'. This gives some idea of the way his voice was initially received: this was not about the discovery of an exciting new writer, it was about an ordinary citizen who had managed to get their voice heard. This was something different to how the more obviously literary Pasternak was viewed. Solzhenitsyn's was the true voice of dissidence, straight from the prison cell. He was known as Russia's conscience, the man who had carried the truth about the camps out 'on the skin of my back'.

The great strength of *One Day in the Life of Ivan Denisovich* is that it parachutes you straight into the world of the camp prisoner, with Alyosha the Baptist (from Alexey, diminutive fans) and Ivan Buinovsky, the ex-naval captain, as your bunkmates. The writing is immediate, diary-like and detailed. Because it focuses on one day – to illustrate the fact that every day is very much like the next – Solzhenitsyn can afford to zoom in on the minutiae of camp life: the sorry patch of fabric with a number sewn on which hangs off a spot on his trousers just above the left knee; the milky-white liquid in the thermometer that never quite seems to dip below minus 41 degrees (the point at which camp labour is called off); the 'putrid little bits of fish' underneath the leaves of boiled black cabbage. This is the opposite of a bird's-eye view. All Ivan Denisovich can see are the things within his immediate vicinity; ideally, below him. It's the account of someone whose head is bowed.

His spirit, though, is not broken: he has found a way to survive in these quashed circumstances. There are systems to follow (store your boots in the right place, don't eat your bread until later in the day) and rules to be observed (take your hat off to a guard five paces before passing him and replace it two paces after). Through Ivan Denisovich, Solzhenitsyn opens up the world of the *zek* (political prisoner). Ivan Denisovich has no reason to be in prison. He knows it, and he suspects his captors know it. Having fought in the Second World War, he was taken prisoner by the Germans. He admits this instead of concealing it. And so he is accused of being a 'German spy' and is sentenced to ten years' forced labour. (Solzhenitsyn was imprisoned in similar circumstances, from 1945 to 1953, except his 'crime' was to write derogatory remarks about Stalin in a letter. He was convicted of 'anti-Soviet propaganda'.)

The publication of *One Day in the Life of Ivan Denisovich* was personally authorized by Khrushchev, who said, 'There's a Stalinist in each of you. There's even a Stalinist in me. We must root out this evil.' In some ways, Solzhenitsyn's fate was tied to Khrushchev's from then on, which meant that, after 1964, when

Khrushchev was deposed, things were never going to go well for the writer. Solzhenitsyn was declared a 'non-person' again in 1965, and the KGB seized a lot of his work. In the case of Solzhenitsyn, and so many Russian writers, they were often from an early age convinced that it was their 'fate' to catalogue the moral state of their country; they were never prey to the First World problem of writer's block or a crisis of self-esteem. That's surprising in some ways, as you'd think the prospect of a knock on the door by the KGB could go either way. You either think: 'What I have to say is so worth saying it's worth dying for.' (Personally, I am a moral coward and I just don't think I could write under those conditions.) Or you think: 'Really, my writing is not so great, comrades. I just won't do any.' (I see this excuse as attractive.) Clearly, this happened, if not consciously, across the Soviet Union for many decades, because there has not been a huge cache of secret brilliant literature that has been unleashed since the USSR collapsed. Luckily for Solzhenitsyn, he thought things like this: 'It is the artist who realizes that there is a supreme force above him and works gladly away as a small apprentice under God's heaven.' The KGB tried to poison him with a biological weapon (probably ricin) in 1971, which left him severely ill but alive. And they expelled him in 1974.

The New York Times once described Solzhenitsyn as a figure of 'almost biblical moral severity'. You only have to look at a picture of him to see that this hyperbole is possibly an understatement. He was the definition of dour and, despite having many reservations about the Soviet system, having been persecuted under it for many years, as a writer he embodied everything about that most Soviet of definitions, Stakhanovite, no matter which country he was working in. (Stakhanov was a miner who in 1935 was said to have exceeded his day's quota of coal by fourteen times. He became the poster boy for increased productivity.) Solzhenitsyn's method for surviving when things went wrong was to put his nose to the grindstone and write. He produced vast quantities of work and was still writing when he died, at the age of eighty-nine, in 2008. One of my favourite stories comes from when he was living in America and headed off to his shack every day to write for hours on end. At the time, he was extremely infirm. His wife said, 'He hasn't left the house for five years. He's missing a vertebra . . . But every day he sits and works.' That's all you need to know about Solzhenitsyn. He's missing a vertebra. But every day he sits and works.

Now, let's be honest about Solzhenitsyn. He is a literary giant. He is one of the greats. No discussion of Russian literature in the twentieth century is complete without him. If one literary figure embodies the Soviet period, it's him. But no one – and I mean no one – reads him for pleasure, not even, I suspect, himself, as, judging by everything I have read about him, he was not one to indulge in pleasures of almost any sort. Maybe there's a book out there that details his fun side ('Solzhenitsyn's guilty pleasures include mint humbugs and re-runs of *Tom and Jerry*'), but I have yet to find it. He is not the Roald Dahl of Soviet literature. He is completely terrifying in his intensity. If Dostoevsky is a hedgehog and, when I was a bit obsessive, I was a porcupine, then Solzhenitsyn is a giant African porcupine. Like most people, when I first read Solzhenitsyn, I read him because I was compelled to, not out of choice. Most people read Solzhenitsyn out of a sense of duty, and rightly so. His readership continues to grow, years after his death, and years after his writing was directly relevant and hugely urgent. His work endures because we want to understand totalitarianism and, on a more personal and relatable level, we want to experience the intimacy of being a victim of totalitarianism. Which, let's face it, you are much better off doing within the confines of someone else's writing than in real life. Anyway, if you have the slightest interest in Russia, how can you not read a man whose work Brezhnev called 'filthy, anti-Soviet slander'? Brezhnev said this about *The Gulag Archipelago* before he or anyone in his entourage had actually read it, because why would you bother reading a book before pronouncing on it? 'No one has had a chance to read the book, but its essential contents are already known,' said Brezhnev. He could have had a great time writing Amazon reviews.

I had practical reasons, though, for solemnly nodding my way through *One Day in the Life of Ivan Denisovich*. Which is, by the way, the best place to start with Solzhenitsyn's work, and a suitable read for anyone in their late teens, as I was at the time. (This was ten years before I realized I was not Russian but, basically, Jewish. I guess if I had known this all along, I could have just been enjoying myself and reading Woody Allen instead of trying to understand the Gulag. Not that I'm bitter or anything.) When I was preparing for my university interview, I knew that the Russian lecturer would be likely to ask me a) what I knew about Soviet power (real answer: very little, except that Gorbachev has a birthmark) and b) what twentieth-century Russian literature I had read. I knew a fair amount about Tolstoy, Dostoevsky and Chekhov. But I knew that would be seen as a baseline requirement and not impressive enough. I needed to have read something more contemporary. And fast. Enter Solzhenitsyn and a book that is very short (just over a hundred pages), easy to read and a brilliantly graspable guide to some of the darkest aspects of Soviet life. It was the perfect package. I took it to my first university visit with me and read it in my room the night before the interview, shivering under the covers because I couldn't work out how to turn on the heater (and imagining melodramatically and idiotically to myself that this was not unlike the conditions which Ivan Denisovich Shukhov faced as a prisoner).

My plan was a roaring success. Early doors, the interview referenced *Anna Karenina*, *War and Peace*, Chekhov's short stories. I said sage and mature things I didn't really understand about naturalism and symbolism. Then came the question, from the Russian tutor interviewing me, an extraordinary and terrifying woman and, it occurred to me, the first Russian I had encountered face to face. She was like something out of Harry Potter: a cross between Dame Maggie Smith as Professor McGonagall and Madame Maxime, the headmistress of the French girls' school played by a giantess version of Frances de la Tour. Imagine this person crossed with a Russian empress turned ballet instructor and you have a quarter of an idea of the magnitude of this lady. During the interview, the telephone rang, and she picked up the receiver and said things in clipped, terrifying Russian. My jaw was on the floor. It was the closest I had come to being in a Bond film.

She put down the phone, smiled tightly and asked the question I had been waiting for: 'And have you read any more contemporary literature?' It was the coded question that really meant: 'Have you read any Solzhenitsyn?' 'Yes,' I beamed, knowing the right answer. 'Solzhenitsyn.' I pronounced it 'Solzy-nit-sin', as if it were some kind of cough medicine from the Robitussin family, not knowing how to pronounce the 'zh' bit. I didn't blame myself for this or feel bad about it. I mean, who speaks English as a native language and is comfortable saying 'Solzhenitsyn'? (In a headline in the mid-1970s, reporting on one of his anti-Western tirades, the *Daily Mirror* called him 'Solzhenitwit'.) 'And what Solzhenitsyn have you read?' she murmured, pronouncing the name carefully and correctly in an attempt to make me remember it. She stared at the floor, as if already aware of the fact that I was getting in way out of my depth. 'Er, *One Day in the Life of Ivan –*' I didn't know how to pronounce 'Denisovich'. (The stress falls on the second syllable: De-NEES-ovich. It's one of the more melodic patronymics.) '*Ivan Denisovich*,' she smiled. 'And what do you think of it?'

This was a difficult question to answer as, drawing on Brezhnev's inspiring example of holding firm opinions about books without having actually read them, I had only got through about the first ten pages. I knew that it was about a man in the Gulag. I had a very hazy understanding of what the Gulag was. I knew that Solzhenitsyn was important and controversial and anti-Soviet. I suddenly became nervous that the person interviewing me might not be anti-Soviet and so I would be judged for praising that side of his work . . . I needed to say something that would not reveal my ignorance and would show that I was capable of thinking on my feet. Miraculously, I found the answer, taking a huge risk, as it could have been factually wrong: 'It's an extraordinary piece of literature because it occupies the space of an entire novel and yet it really is just about one day in the life of one man.'

I said this slowly and deliberately, as if it were very profound. I genuinely believed it as I said it, as I still think it's a pretty bold and outlandish move to say, 'I know, I'll write a novel about the Gulag. Only I'll just write the whole thing about one day in the life of one man. I can just stretch it out. Who needs to know about what happens over more than twenty-four hours? If it's good enough for *Mrs Dalloway* . . .' And yet, it was also a profoundly stupid thing to say because it was so bloody obvious. And, more crucially, because I hadn't read it, I didn't have any evidence that the novel really did cover only one day (for all I knew, it could have spanned a thousand years and the 'one day' of the title was just part of a flashback). Anyway. Whatever I said was the right thing to say, and I passed the test. The first Groskop in a university. A hundred and thirty years after my great-great-grandfather had first entered the country as a Polish Jew whose descendants later refused to acknowledge or just kind of forgot that he was a Polish Jew. Not that I knew that at the time. Otherwise, I might not have been in a room pretending to know about Solzhenitsyn.

It took me years to return to Solzhenitsyn, having found his work very hard to engage with when I was a student. If one of the great lessons of his work is about continuing doggedly on in the face of great adversity, this is – ironically enough – a lesson you really need to absorb in order to read anything he has ever written. Even his compatriots feel this way. Solzhenitsyn occupies a strange, complicated and sometimes unwelcome place in the minds of Russians. His work is not quite literary and yet it's among some of the greatest literature (perhaps some of the only true literature) of the Soviet period. And yet he's not quite a historian because he's a writer. Neither did he do himself any favours when he returned to Russia as an old man. He held a combination of extremely progressive and extremely reactionary views, much of them rooted, Tolstoy-style, in spirituality, morality and the Orthodox Church. Much like Tolstoy, he would perhaps have been better suited to a life as a monk than a life as a writer forced to take on the status quo.

One episode that illustrates perfectly the trouble with Solzhenitsyn is the theme of the speech he gave as a Commencement Address at Harvard University in 1978, when he had settled in the United States. Bearing in mind that he's a Soviet exile and one of the greatest writers in the world, to be fair, it can't have been easy to know what to talk about that would move his audience. So what does he choose as his engaging, crowd-pleasing topic? 'Anthropocentrism in Modern Western Culture'. This is just a fancy way of saying that we care more about humans than we care about nature and the planet (and he has a very good point). But it strikes me as typically provocative of Solzhenitsyn. He can't quite bring himself to be anti-Soviet. And so he finds another way of attacking the West: 'Don't be smug, you guys! You are obsessed with yourselves!' And he launches it upon people with a fancy-schmancy annoying title. This could be a very brave thing to do. But it strikes me as incredibly pompous and self-serving, and it's one of the reasons I couldn't get along with Solzhenitsyn as a personality for a long time.

I have, however, become fond of him because of his extreme, uncompromising reputation. In short, everyone should love Solzhenitsyn, because he was hardcore. Remember the missing vertebra. He did not just write about how to survive adversity, he lived it out, even when he was not facing that much adversity any more. There is no account of him ever having taken a day off, or a holiday. The tales of his time living in America illustrate this. The locals there protected his privacy, which meant everything to him. The nearby grocery store, Joe Allan's, was famous for its handwritten sign: 'No Directions to the Solzhenitsyns'. After his death, in 2008, his former neighbours in Vermont reported that he had been 'fairly enigmatic'. He was rarely interviewed while he lived in the US. His opinion was much sought during the period of perestroika and glasnost in the late 1980s, but he simply shrugged and said there was not much point in saying anything because things were moving so quickly that any opinion would soon be outdated. He was once interviewed by the local magazine *Vermont Life*, which reported that he seemed to work 24/7 and that the light in his writer's cabin never went out. A local doctor who treated Solzhenitsyn's children said, 'No matter how late it was, he seemed to be working.' (I love that 'seemed'. It would have been great if he was actually watching cartoons. Unlikely, unfortunately. More likely, he was trying to crush another vertebra.) As the Russian journalist Vitali Vitaliev has reported, Solzhenitsyn kept regular hours and did so religiously: from 8 a.m. to 10 p.m. every day for seventeen years, supposedly without a day off. Sometimes, he broke off to hit a ball across the adjacent tennis court. Wild.

This kind of regime cannot be maintained without the support of a spouse. One of my favourite lines in *One Day in the Life of Ivan Denisovich* reveals Solzhenitsyn's attitude towards women, which is typical of his time, but there is perhaps some self-awareness there, too. (Perhaps. I'm being generous.) When Ivan Denisovich describes the making up of his bed, how he tries to keep it clean, how he sews a hunk of bread into his mattress where no one can steal it, he marvels at how unnecessarily intricate bedlinen is outside prison. Why would you bother with all that when you can just put a blanket on a mattress? He writes: ' . . . it even seemed odd for women to bother about sheets, all that extra laundering.' (Women! They're so crazy! They make you put sheets on the bed!) Of course, outside prison, it's the women who bother with everything, who look after you and keep your life running. This was pretty much Solzhenitsyn's experience of life. I remember reading an interview with his second wife, the one who went to the US with him, in which she explained that Solzhenitsyn was a person who never answered the telephone because she would always answer it for him. That is how you get a lot of writing done.

Solzhenitsyn's first wife gave some extraordinary interviews about their life together before he became famous. She also spoke awkwardly about his second marriage, adding that at least it was easy for him not to forget his second wife's name, as they were both called Natalia. (I know it's wrong to be entertained by this. But it's funny.) I have a lot of sympathy for everyone involved here, as it must have been awful to live through: the KGB 'sponsored' a series of books denouncing Solzhenitsyn, one of which was a memoir which went out under his first wife's name. He and those close to him were subjected to a constant campaign of intimidation.

I think, underneath it all, Solzhenitsyn was a kind-hearted man. The immense personal price he paid in order to keep writing is unimaginable. He was always scribbling away in tiny notebooks and transcribing things and hiding them and burning bits of manuscript in a bonfire in the garden so that the KGB wouldn't find them. What sort of person would you become in these circumstances? When the writer Lydia Chukovskaya was interviewed by David Remnick of the *New Yorker* about her friendship with Solzhenitsyn in the early 1970s, she told him how they would keep similar writing hours and he would be anxious not to disturb her. He would leave notes on the fridge that said things like: 'If you are free at nine, let's listen to the radio together.' That is resilience. I was going to need a lot of it to overcome my irritation that I was not Russian. I felt like I'd had a vertebra removed. But, unlike Solzhenitsyn, the pain didn't motivate me. Instead of carrying on, I felt like collapsing.

9. How to Have a Sense of Humour about Life: *The Master and Margarita* by Mikhail Bulgakov

(Or: *Don't get run over by a tram after talking to Satan*)

'"And what is your particular field of work?" asked Berlioz.
"I specialise in black magic.""

If many Russian classics are dark and deep and full of the horrors of the blackness of the human soul (or, indeed, are about the Gulag), then this is the one book to buck the trend. Of all the Russian classics, *The Master and Margarita* is undoubtedly the most cheering. It's funny, it's profound and it has to be read to be believed. In some ways, the book has an odd reputation. It is widely acknowledged as one of the greatest novels of the twentieth century and as a masterpiece of magical realism, but it's very common even for people who are very well read not to have heard of it, although among Russians you have only to mention a cat the size of a pig and apricot juice that makes you hiccup and everyone will know what you are talking about. Most of all, it is the book that saved me when I felt like I had wasted my life. It's a novel that encourages you not to take yourself too seriously, no matter how bad things have got. *The Master and Margarita* is a reminder that, ultimately, everything is better if you can inject a note of silliness and of the absurd. Not only is this a possibility at any time; occasionally, it's an absolute necessity: 'You've got to laugh. Otherwise you'd cry.'

For those who already know and love *The Master and Margarita*, there is something of a cult-like 'circle of trust' thing going on. I've formed friendships with people purely on the strength of the knowledge that they have read and enjoyed this novel. I have a friend who married her husband almost exclusively because he told her he had read it. I would normally say that it's not a great idea to found a lifelong relationship on the basis of liking one particular book. But, in this case, it's a very special book. So, if you are unmarried, and you love it and you meet someone else who loves it, you should definitely marry them. It's the most entertaining and comforting novel. When I was feeling low about not being able to pretend to be Russian any more, I would read bits of it to cheer myself up and remind myself that, whatever the truth about where I come from, I had succeeded in understanding some important things about another culture. It is a book that takes your breath away and makes you laugh out loud, sometimes at its cleverness, sometimes because it's just so funny and ridiculous. I might have kidded myself that you need to be a bit Russian to understand Tolstoy. But with Bulgakov, all you need to understand him is a sense of humour. His comedy is universal.

Written in the 1930s but not published until the 1960s, *The Master and Margarita* is the most breathtakingly original piece of work. Few books can match it for weirdness. The devil, Woland, comes to Moscow with a retinue of terrifying henchmen, including, of course, the giant talking cat (literally 'the size of a pig'), a witch and a wall-eyed assassin with one yellow fang. They appear to be targeting Moscow's literary elite. Woland meets Berlioz, influential magazine editor and chairman of the biggest Soviet writers' club. (Berlioz has been drinking the hiccup-inducing apricot juice.) Berlioz believes Woland to be some kind of German professor. Woland predicts Berlioz's death, which almost instantly comes to pass when the editor is decapitated in a freak accident involving a tram and a spillage of sunflower oil. All this happens within the first few pages.

A young poet, Ivan Bezdomny (his surname means 'Homeless'), has witnessed this incident and heard Woland telling a bizarre story about Pontius Pilate. (This 'Procurator of Judaea' narrative is interspersed between the 'Moscow' chapters.) Bezdomny attempts to chase Woland and his gang but ends up in a lunatic asylum, ranting about an evil professor who is obsessed with Pontius Pilate. In the asylum, he meets the Master, a writer who has been locked away for writing a novel about Jesus Christ and, yes, Pontius Pilate. The story of the relationship between Christ and Pilate, witnessed by Woland and recounted by the Master, returns at intervals throughout the novel and, eventually, both stories tie in together. (Stick with me here. Honestly, it's big fun.)

Meanwhile, outside the asylum, Woland has taken over Berlioz's flat and is hosting magic shows for Moscow's elite. He summons the Master's mistress, Margarita, who has remained loyal to the writer and his work. At a midnight ball hosted by Satan, Woland offers Margarita the chance to become a witch with magical powers. This happens on Good Friday, the day Christ is crucified. (Seriously, all this makes perfect sense when you are reading the book. And it is not remotely confusing. I promise.) At the ball, there is a lot of naked dancing and cavorting (oh, suddenly you're interested and want to read this book?) and then Margarita starts flying around naked, first across Moscow and then the USSR. Again, I repeat: this all makes sense within the context of the book.

Woland grants Margarita one wish. She chooses the most altruistic thing possible, liberating a woman she meets at the ball from eternal suffering. The devil decides not to count this wish and gives her another one. This time, Margarita chooses to free the Master. Woland is not happy about this and gets her and the Master to drink poisoned wine. They come together again in the afterlife, granted 'peace' but not 'light', a limbo situation that has caused academics to wrap themselves up in knots for years. Why doesn't Bulgakov absolve them? Why do both Jesus and the Devil seem to agree on their punishment? Bulgakov seems to suggest that you should always choose freedom – but expect it to come at a price.

One of the great strengths of *The Master and Margarita* is its lightness of tone. It's full of cheap (but good) jokes at the expense of the literati, who get their comeuppance for rejecting the Master's work. (This is a parallel of Bulgakov's experience; he was held at arm's length by the Soviet literary establishment and 'allowed' to work only in the theatre, and even then with some difficulty). In dealing so frivolously and surreally with the nightmare society in which Woland wreaks havoc, Bulgakov's satire becomes vicious without even needing to draw blood. His characters are in a sort of living hell, but they never quite lose sight of the fact that entertaining and amusing things are happening around them. However darkly comedic these things might sometimes be.

While *The Master and Margarita* is a hugely complex novel, with its quasi-religious themes and its biting critique of the Soviet system, above all it's a big fat lesson in optimism through laughs. If you can't see the funny side of your predicament, then what is the point of anything? Bulgakov loves to make fun of everyone and everything. 'There's only one way a man can walk round Moscow in his underwear – when he's being escorted by the police on the way to a police station!' (This is when Ivan Bezdomny appears, half naked, at the writers' restaurant to tell them a strange character has come to Moscow and murdered their colleague.) 'I'd rather be a tram conductor and there's no job worse than that.' (The giant cat talking rubbish at Satan's ball.) 'The only thing that can save a mortally wounded cat is a drink of paraffin.' (More cat gibberish.)

The final joke of the book is that maybe Satan is not the bad guy after all. While I was trying to recover my sense of humour about being Polish and Jewish instead of being Russian, this was all a great comfort. Life is, in Bulgakov's eyes, a great cosmic joke. Of course, there's a political message here, too. But Bulgakov delivers it with such gusto and playfulness that you never feel preached at. You have got to be a seriously good satirist in order to write a novel where the Devil is supposed to represent Stalin and/or Soviet power without making the reader feel you are bludgeoning them over the head with the idea. Bulgakov's novel is tragic and poignant in many ways, but this feeling sneaks up on you only afterwards. Most of all, Bulgakov is about conjuring up a feeling of fun. Perhaps because of this he's the cleverest and most subversive of all the writers who were working at this time. It's almost impossible to believe that he and Pasternak were contemporaries, so different are their novels in style and tone. (Pasternak was born in 1890, Bulgakov in 1891.) *The Master and Margarita* and *Doctor Zhivago* feel as if they were written in two different centuries.

Unlike Pasternak, though, Bulgakov never experienced any reaction to his novel during his lifetime, as it wasn't published until after he had died. One of the things that makes *The Master and Margarita* so compelling is the circumstances in which it was written. Bulgakov wrote it perhaps not only 'for the drawer' (i.e. not to be published within his lifetime) but never to be read by anyone at all. He was writing it at a time of Black Marias (the KGB's fleet of cars), knocks on the door and disappearances in the middle of the night. Ordinary life had been turned on its head for most Muscovites, and yet they had to find a way to keep on living and pretending that things were normal. Bulgakov draws on this and creates a twilight world where nothing is as it seems and the fantastical, paranormal and downright evil are treated as everyday occurrences.

It's hard to imagine how Bulgakov would have survived if the novel had been released. Bulgakov must have known this when he was writing it. And he also must have known that it could never be published – which means that he did not hold back and wrote exactly what he wanted, without fear of retribution. (Although there was always the fear that the novel would be discovered. Just to write it would have been a crime, let alone to attempt to have it published.) This doesn't mean that he in any way lived a carefree life. He worried about being attacked by the authorities. He worried about being prevented from doing any work that would earn him money. He worried about being unable to finish this novel. And he worried incessantly – and justifiably – about his health.

During his lifetime Bulgakov was known for his dystopian stories 'The Fatal Eggs' (1924) and 'The Heart of a Dog' (1925) and his play *The Days of the Turbins* (1926), about the civil war. Despite his early success, from his late twenties onwards, Bulgakov seemed to live with an awareness that he was probably going to be cut down in mid-life. He wrote a note to himself on the manuscript of *The Master and Margarita* : 'Finish it before you die.' J. A. E. Curtis's compelling biography *Manuscripts Don't Burn: Mikhail Bulgakov, A Life in Letters and Diaries*, gives a near-cinematic insight into the traumatic double life Bulgakov was leading as he wrote the novel in secrecy. I love this book with the same intensity that I love *The Master and Margarita*. Curtis's quotes from the letters and the diaries bring Bulgakov to life and are packed full of black comedy and everyday detail, from Bulgakov begging his brother not to send coffee and socks from Paris because 'the duty has gone up considerably' to his wife's diary entry from New Year's Day 1937 which tells of Bulgakov's joy at smashing cups with 1936 written on them.

As well as being terrified that he would never finish *The Master and Margarita*, Bulgakov was becoming increasingly ill. In 1934, he wrote to a friend that he had been suffering from insomnia, weakness and 'finally, which was the filthiest thing I have ever experienced in my life, a fear of solitude, or to be more precise, a fear of being left on my own. It's so repellent that I would prefer to have a leg cut off.' He was often in physical pain with a kidney disease but was just as tortured psychologically. There was the continual business of seeming to be offered the chance to travel abroad, only for it to be withdrawn. Of course, the authorities had no interest in letting him go, in case he never came back. (Because it would make them look bad if talented writers didn't want to live in the USSR. And because it was much more fun to keep them in their own country, attempt to get them to write things praising Soviet power and torture them, in most cases literally.)

It is extraordinary that Bulgakov managed to write a novel that is so full of humour and wit and lightness of tone when he was living through this period. He grew accustomed to being in a world where sometimes the phone would ring, he would pick it up and on the other end of the line an anonymous official would say something like: 'Go to the Foreign Section of the Executive Committee and fill in a form for yourself and your wife.' He would do this and grow cautiously hopeful. And then, instead of an international passport, he would receive a slip of paper that read: 'M. A. Bulgakov is refused permission.' In all the years that Bulgakov continued, secretly, to write *The Master and Margarita* – as well as making a living (of sorts) as a playwright – what is ultimately surprising is that he did not go completely insane from all the cat-and-mouse games that Stalin and his acolytes played with him. Stalin took a personal interest in him, in the same way he did with Akhmatova. There's some suggestion that his relationship with Stalin prevented Bulgakov's arrest and execution. But it also prevented him from being able to work on anything publicly he wanted to work on.

How galling, too, to have no recognition in your own lifetime for your greatest work. When the book did come out in 1966–7, its significance was immense, perhaps greater than any other book published in the twentieth century. As the novelist Viktor Pelevin once said, it's almost impossible to explain to anyone who has not lived through Soviet life exactly what this novel meant to people. '*The Master and Margarita* didn't even bother to be anti-Soviet, yet reading this book would make you free instantly. It didn't liberate you from some particular old ideas, but rather from the hypnotism of the entire order of things.'

The Master and Margarita symbolizes dissidence; it's a wry acknowledgement that bad things happened that can never, ever be forgiven. But it is also representative of an interesting kind of passivity or non-aggression. It is not a novel that encourages revolution. It is a novel that throws its hands up in horror but does not necessarily know what to do next. Literature can be a catalyst for change. But it can also be a safety valve for a release of tension and one that results in paralysis. I sometimes wonder if *The Master and Margarita* – the novel I have heard Russians speak the most passionately about – explains many Russians' indifference to politics and current affairs. They are deeply cynical, for reasons explored fully in this novel. Bulgakov describes a society where nothing is as it seems. People lie routinely. People who do not deserve them receive rewards. You can be declared insane simply for wanting to write fiction. *The Master and Margarita* is, ultimately, a huge study in cognitive dissonance. It's about a state of mind where nothing adds up and yet you must act as if it does. Often, the only way to survive in that state is to tune out. And, ideally, make a lot of jokes about how terrible everything is.

Overtly, Bulgakov also wants us to think about good and evil, light and darkness. So as not to be preachy about things, he does this by mixing in absurd humour. Do you choose to be the sort of person who joins Woland's retinue of weirdos? (Wall-eyed goons, step forward!) Or do you choose to be the sort of person who is prepared to go to an insane asylum for writing poetry? (I didn't say these were straightforward choices.) On a deeper level, he is asking whether we are okay with standing up for what we believe in, even if the consequences are terrifying. And he is challenging us to live a life where we can look ourselves in the eye and be happy with who we are. There is always a light in the dark. But first, you have to be the right kind of person to be able to see it.

The Master and Margarita is so fantastical that many aspects of it cannot possibly be autobiographical, however much I would like to have discovered that Bulgakov owned a really fat, massive cat. But some scenes are drawn from real life. There is a suggestion that Bulgakov must have based some of the ball scenes in the novel on a legendary party he and his wife, Yelena Sergeyevna, were invited to at the American embassy in 1935. She writes in her diary that they went to a special imported-goods shop and bought 'English' fabric which cost twenty-five gold roubles a length to have tails made for Bulgakov. She wears an evening dress of 'rippling dark blue with pale pink flowers' and has two people round to dress her, the seamstress and a friend. The party itself sounds amazing. Next to the orchestra is a section cordoned off with a net which houses 'live pheasants and other birds'. In the dining room there are 'live bear-cubs in one corner, kid goats, and cockerels in cages'. On the top floor, where Kazakh dancers are performing, they have set up a kebab stand. According to one account, the bear was not house-trained and befouled a general's uniform.

At the time, Bulgakov had tried to befriend various American embassy types in his attempts to travel abroad. One of my favourite diary entries in *Manuscripts Don't Burn* comes from the occasion when one of them invites Bulgakov for lunch. 'Before the meal we were served cocktails,' he writes. Then he adds: 'The meal was without soup.' Both the diaries and the letters of Bulgakov and his wife are full of good-humoured anecdotes about their attempts to maintain a decent, middle-class life in the face of the system's attempts to hobble Bulgakov as a writer. Yelena writes: 'Yesterday, quite by chance – an American was moving out of our block – I bought Misha a very elegant and original-looking fur-coat for a thousand roubles. The fur is grey – American grizzly bear.'

The figure of Margarita was also, to some extent, drawn from life: she is based on Yelena Sergeyevna. The story of how Bulgakov and his 'real-life Margarita' met is like something out of a fantastical novel itself. When they first came across each other in 1929, she was married to a lieutenant general and had two young sons. (Bulgakov had already been married twice.) At this first encounter, however, she knew, Russian-style, that this was her fate. She initially avoided the relationship, refusing to leave the house or answer any phone calls or letters from him. Supposedly, a year and a half later, having not set foot out of the house in all that time (I find this bit hard to believe), she ran into Bulgakov in the street and he told her, 'I can't live without you.'

They married in 1932 and had eight years together before Bulgakov died from a kidney disorder inherited from his father. Their time together was difficult because Bulgakov was under intense scrutiny. They tried to put a brave face on things and sometimes seemed to fake a 'let them eat cake' mentality in the face of despair. Another diary entry from Yelena Sergeyevna: 'For supper we had caviar, smoked salmon, home-made pâté, radishes, fresh cucumbers, fried mushrooms, vodka and white wine.' They invite friends out to 'the club' for *pelmeni* (dumplings – think soggy ravioli) and go to performances of Prokofiev and Shostakovich ('without noticing it we drank three bottles of champagne'). When Bulgakov was told that if he didn't write a propaganda play when it was demanded of him, his most successful play would be withdrawn from the theatre, he replied: 'Oh well, I shall have to sell the chandelier.' Later,

Yelena Sergeyevna writes: 'We are 17 thousand [roubles] in debt and don't have a kopek of current income.'

Bulgakov could have a real Noël Coward quality about him. On the tenth-anniversary performance of his play *The Days of the Turbins*, there is no celebration. 'Needless to say, it didn't even occur to the Theatre to mark it in any way,' Yelena Sergeyevna writes. Bulgakov pens a letter imagining an anniversary present from the theatre producers: 'The valuable gift will take the form of a large saucepan made of some precious metal (copper, for example), filled with all the blood they have sucked from me over the ten years.' In 1937, he notes in a letter to a friend that 'well-wishers' have started to say to him, 'Never mind, it will all get printed after your death.' 'I am very grateful to them, of course!' he jokes.

He celebrated the success of his plays but hated taking a bow on stage. He was endlessly tormented by the director Stanislavsky rehearsing his plays but never staging them, and he found it exceedingly irritating that, whenever he went to the rehearsal, the actors were not going over the scenes but were being lectured by Stanislavsky about some completely random and unrelated thing. When at last his play *Molière* premiered (this was one that Stanislavsky rehearsed for four years), it received twenty-two curtain calls. But it also had four significant negative reviews and within six weeks had been cancelled, after a final, unsigned article in *Pravda* finished it off. The headline? 'Superficial Glitter and False Content'. Can you imagine having your play rehearsed for four years, it getting twenty-two curtain calls and then having to close within six weeks? Bulgakov's state of mind doesn't bear thinking about.

But Bulgakov likened the idea of a writer not writing to expecting someone to give up sex. 'Supposing a man has been told, "You can't have children." Then he says to himself, "So what's the point of having sexual relations. To hell with it!" And then a monstrous thing happens: his health goes to pieces, he is consumed with exasperation and frustration, he sees naked girls in his sleep and can't think of anything else. Is an artist's desire to write any weaker than sexual desire?' He struggled to resign himself to his fate and suffered bitterly. He wrote in his diary in 1922: 'My wife and I are starving. The other day I had to ask my uncle to help us with some flour, oil and potatoes.' He complained to writer friends that he couldn't write to them in ink because he couldn't afford it: only in scratchy pencil. In 1929, he wrote to his brother: 'All my plays have been banned and not a single line of my fiction has been published. Bulgakov, the writer, is dead.' And in 1930: 'I am doomed to remain silent and possibly starve.'

The interactions with Stalin became progressively worse. Bulgakov first came to Stalin's attention as a result of his play *The Days of the Turbins*, a theatrical adaptation of his novel *The White Guard*. The play was savaged by the Soviet critics, who were horrified that it sympathized with White officers. But Stalin saw this ultimately as a compliment (or at least he pretended to – possibly, he was already toying with Bulgakov), claiming that to show the White officers as decent people and still depict them as defeated losers was in fact a great tribute to Soviet power. It was 'a demonstration of the crushing power of Bolshevism'. (Hmm. Sounds like a play you'd really like to go and see, right?) Stalin was very weird about the things that he liked (surprise!) and the things that he liked to pronounce on. He went to see this play fifteen times.

This did not help Bulgakov; if anything, the opposite. By 1929, his work had been banned. And by 1930, he was writing a letter to Stalin asking for his permission to emigrate. Stalin telephoned Bulgakov and, again, not really supporting him, more likely playing with him, gave him a job at the Moscow Art Theatre. On 18 April 1930, Bulgakov had a phone call from Stalin, having written to him to explain that he needed work or permission to leave the country. Stalin: 'Is it true that you want to leave the country? Are we really so disgusting to you?' It is thought that this phone call was motivated by the suicide of the poet Mayakovsky. To some extent, the state needed Bulgakov – or, at least, they needed to be able to pretend that he wasn't unhappy with the idea of Soviet power.

There is so much to like about Bulgakov. As Ellendea Proffer relates in her biography, his colleagues on a literary magazine noted that he was so old-school that it antagonized people. He wore his fur coat (which was seen as bourgeois). He kissed women's hands. He bowed. The crease in his trousers was always pressed just so. When trying to recover from illness on holiday in Sukhumi on the Black Sea, he wrote that he was eating only rice pudding and bilberry jelly because the hotel food was 'complete rubbish' like beef stroganoff. He used to send his wife letters that said things like 'Musya! [one of his many pet diminutives for her] I've never eaten anything so delightful. Thank you for a marvellous supper.' In another letter when they are apart, he writes about some insect bites on his foot that are annoying him: 'I've just realized that I'm writing nonsense! It must be very interesting to read about the sole of my foot! I'm sorry.'

As recounted in the diaries in *Manuscripts Don't Burn*, at one point Yelena's sister takes over the typing up of *The Master and Margarita*, and she absolutely hates the book. Her experience of being one of the first readers of the greatest novel of the twentieth century is not a happy one. She tells Bulgakov she has told her husband she 'can't see the main direction in the novel'. This, Bulgakov notes, is twenty-two chapters in. If she doesn't get it now, she's never going to get it. 'In the course of 327 pages she smiled once, on page 245 ("Glorious sea . . ."). Why that precisely should amuse her I do not know. I am not confident that she will ever succeed in discovering any sort of main direction in the novel, but on the other hand I am certain that utter disapproval of the work on her part has been guaranteed.' She told him, damningly: 'This novel is your own private affair.' (This is a very Russian thing to say. A bit like saying in English: 'Well, it's up to you . . .' when clearly what you mean to say is: 'This is mad and a very bad idea.')

In his final year alive, there was a terrible brush with Stalin. Bulgakov wrote what was to be his last letter to him, to intercede on behalf of his friend the playwright Nikolai Erdman. (This particular intervention didn't get Erdman what he wanted, but he later won the Stalin Prize and lived until 1970.) Bulgakov was then working on *Batumi*, a play that had been commissioned for Stalin's sixtieth birthday, which fell at the end of 1939. (Batumi is a resort in Georgia where Stalin had spent some of his youth.) It later transpired that there was some confusion over Stalin's birthdate, which he changed at least once. It now seems more likely that he turned sixty in 1938. Which makes it even more annoying that Bulgakov was being forced to work on a play he didn't want to work on to celebrate a birthday on the wrong day and in the wrong year. (Welcome to Soviet power.)

It's hard to understand why Bulgakov would take on such a play. You have to wonder what he thought the best-case scenario was. Possibly, he felt threatened and unable to say no. Possibly, he was intrigued and wanted to challenge himself. Going by his letters and diaries, it was probably a bit of both. Or perhaps he would have done anything to get a bit of extra time and money so that he could work on the secret manuscript of *The Master and Margarita*.

As the play was being prepared, a team from the Moscow Art Theatre was sent to Batumi in August 1939. On the way there, they received news that Stalin did not want the play to be performed. Bulgakov would have been notified shortly after the killing of Zinaida Reich, the wife of the playwright Vsevolod Meyerhold. She was an exceptionally beautiful actress who was killed in her apartment, aged forty-five, stabbed seventeen times (including directly in her eyes) by two attackers believed to be from the NKVD (later the KGB). First, this was someone known to Bulgakov and his wife. Second, this was a sign that no one was safe. Three years before, Meyerhold had written an attack on Bulgakov's work in a theatre magazine. If anything, Meyerhold was less subversive than Bulgakov and should have been better protected from the regime.

Some of the saddest bits in the Bulgakov letters and diaries are where his wife writes in a tragic Disgusted-of-Tunbridge-Wells sort of way: 'Misha is considering writing a letter to the authorities.' A strongly worded letter, surely! This is after seventeen of his works have been suppressed over a ten-year period, he is drowning in debt and self-loathing, he has burned loads of his manuscripts and he is suffering from a terminal illness. It's the Englishness of the Bulgakovs' life that I love and which also breaks my heart. They don't want to complain too much. They occasionally buy some nice clothes to cheer themselves up. They make a special note in their diaries when they eat something rather delicious. They consider writing somewhat brusque letters to Stalin (but don't actually write or send all of them, at least not in the latter years). They have quietly and politely given up, without quite admitting it to themselves. And yet, somehow, they keep going, Bulgakov continues writing and his wife's sister carries on, sceptically and resentfully, typing up the novel that she thinks is so rubbish it's embarrassing. They try hard – so hard! – to keep their sense of humour.

Even in the final months of his life, Bulgakov manages a wry smile when the sanatorium staff put him on a 'blended' diet. 'Mostly vegetables in all forms, and fruits. The one and the other are fearfully dull . . . And anyway it's so important for me to be able to read and write that I am even prepared to chew such rubbish as carrots.' By this point, his eyesight is failing and he knows that his kidneys are packing up. Still, he jokes: 'As you know, there is only one decent way of dying, and that is with the help of a firearm, but unfortunately I do not possess such a thing.' Laughing, always, even when life is at its blackest. Perhaps especially when it is at its blackest.

Bulgakov may not quite have realized it himself, but it was his sense of humour that kept him alive. He has a take on things that feels modern and fresh. (Think Woody Allen: 'I'm not afraid of death; I just don't want to be there when it happens.') Here was a brilliant satirist who, because of censorship, was unable to find an audience for his jokes during his lifetime. And he was living through a moment in history which was so close to a joke that it was almost beyond parody. And yet he secretly found a way to bring it to life, in the pages of a book dominated by Satan. Bulgakov had something of the jester about him until the last, as Akhmatova suggests in the poem she wrote for him after his death:

> I offer this to you in place of graveside roses,
> Instead of smoking incense;
> You lived so severely, and to the end you carried
> Your magnificent disdain.
> You drank wine, you were an incomparable jester,
> And gasped for breath between stifling walls,
> And you yourself let in your awesome guest,
> And with her you remained alone.

10. How to Avoid Hypocrisy: *Dead Souls* by Nikolai Gogol

(Or: Don't buy non-existent peasants as part of a get-rich-quick scheme)

'Just let me forget it and not know anything
about it and then I'll be happy.'

Once the whole 'Russian' thing collapsed, I backed away from Russia for a while. It helped that my life had changed radically in the meantime. I now had three children. Very occasionally, I would meet people and they would say, 'Oh, you speak Russian! How marvellous! Do your children speak Russian?' And I would see the lie I had told myself. You are only really 'from' somewhere if you want to speak to your children in that language. That would never have been the case. 'I think it would be a bit pretentious to talk to them in a language that isn't my native language,' I would reply weakly, taking the small-talk question too seriously. 'Oh, that's a shame for them. It would give them such an advantage,' the person would say brightly. And what advantage exactly would that be? So they could pretend they were Russian too, and then find out they weren't?

Into my mid-thirties, a part of me clung on to the idea that I could still incorporate Russian things into my life. But this plan was becoming more theoretical with every baby that came along. Nonetheless, with each of my children, I took them on assignment to places which were really inappropriate: to Odessa, to Moscow. There were moments when I thought, 'Do I really want to be doing this?' I can remember changing a nappy on the

173

floor of an art gallery in Moscow, waiting to do an interview with the novelist Ludmilla Petrushevskaya for a newspaper. I was happy to be there and doing what I wanted to do. But I couldn't help thinking: 'Hmm. I wish I was at home on maternity leave.' Of course, if I had been at home on maternity leave, I would have been sitting in front of daytime television lactating and weeping about why I wasn't on assignment in Russia. It was like I was inside my own version of *Three Sisters*, only actually in Moscow, wishing that I was not in Moscow. Or, as Solzhenitsyn's Ivan Denisovich would say: we always think the other person is holding a bigger radish in their hand. I was always in the wrong place, wishing that I was holding a different variety of radish.

Eventually, though, I had to reconcile myself to the fact that I had enough home-grown produce of my own to be getting on with. And my radishes were not Russian radishes. They were English radishes. My children were a great reminder of this. They, very sensibly, have no desire to learn Russian, even though they are occasionally amused to hear me speak it. And why should they? They know what their roots are and, knowing them, are not especially obsessed with them. The reason I was obsessed was because I was in the dark. Now that things were out in the light, it didn't grip me quite as much. Strangely, I didn't have an overwhelming desire to visit Łódź, where my ancestors came from. In fact, instead I became gradually more conscious – and embarrassed – by the fact that I'd completely overlooked my mother's roots in Northern Ireland in favour of something more foreign and alienating.

And yet, without being Russian, things had turned out in such a way that I have this wonderful connection to Russian because I have studied it for so long and because it has been so close to my heart all this time. I almost feel as if this is a better connection than one that occurs by birth. Russian is not family for me. You can't choose family. But it is a very good lifelong friend. They say friends can be better than family sometimes. Because you choose your friends. This is a friend I chose by accident and decided to stick with.

All the same, there was something hideous about what I had done. I'd allowed myself to get carried away with a romantic idea. It was self-involved and even a bit pompous. I had made myself into a Gogolian caricature: a grotesque, the English country girl who fancies herself more exotic than she really is. The only comfort to me once I began to realize this was the thought that human beings are essentially stupid and we all do incredibly foolish things all the time and it's not even necessarily that unattractive, which is why we don't see the stupidity of the behaviour when we're doing it. The appeal of Chichikov, the horrible anti-hero of *Dead Souls* who buys non-existent serfs to make himself look like a landed gent, is his chutzpah. He breezes through life as if he's touched by stardust. Sometimes, we quite like people who are arrogant or self-serving – if their charade is entertaining enough. I'd have had to have a lot of chutzpah to pass myself off as Russian. Now, the mask was off.

Gogol warns that it's one thing to fool others and another to fool ourselves. We frequently pretend that we're being 'honest' or 'open' when in fact we're doing something for our own benefit. I had pretended to myself that I was studying my Russian roots for the sake of authenticity. But it had been anything but authentic: it was a fiction I had invented for myself. Similarly, Chichikov argues that he's 'helping' others by acquiring their 'dead souls'. Really, all he wants is for everyone to see him as rich and powerful. Hypocrisy is an easy trap to fall into: we convince ourselves so easily that we're doing the right thing because we don't want to see that we're doing the convenient thing – or the thing that just makes us feel better about ourselves.

While being undeniably Russian, *Dead Souls* comes across as the most English of all the Russian novels. It has a Dickensian feel to it, with characters who are reminiscent of Wilkins Micawber, Uriah Heep or Miss Havisham. A mysterious stranger called Chichikov arrives in the town of N—. He visits a series of landowners, making an identical offer to each of them: he would like to purchase the names of any dead serfs they have registered on the census. This doesn't seem like a bad deal. If they 'sell' the 'dead souls', the landowners can stop paying tax against the serfs who have died on them. (As one landlady explains: 'The people are dead, but you've got to pay like they're alive.') And Chichikov can 'own' many serfs, thereby reinventing himself as an aristocrat. What could possibly go wrong? Except, of course, that this is a phantom transaction, involving the transfer of the names of dead people from one man's ownership to another. It's essentially a meaningless deal. But if it means so much to Chichikov and he's willing to go along with it and front up the money . . .? Well, why wouldn't you?

Chichikov's victims are, of course, initially sceptical. ('Really, my dear sir, I've never yet had occasion to sell deceased folk.') They are caught between wondering whether this offer is too good to be true and thinking to themselves that they must be able to get a better deal elsewhere if this man is willing to pay so much for so little. But, like the landlady who has no list of her dead serfs except in her head (and even then seems to know them only by a series of made-up names: 'Don't-Respect-the-Feeding-Trough', 'Cow-Brick' and, my favourite, 'Ivan the Wheel'), they all give in eventually to Chichikov's smooth talk.

Dead Souls was seen to be a controversial and mysterious title. Gogol also insisted on giving it the rather strange and unnecessary subtitle 'Poema' – 'An Epic Poem'. He added this as if to underline that it is not a novel, it is something more than that. Or perhaps he meant it ironically, or satirically. There is a lot of disagreement on this point. Of course, it's not a poem in the usual sense of a poem, it's very clearly a novel, and a fairly conventional episodic novel at that. We are meant to think it is like Homer's *Odyssey* or Dante's *Inferno*.

One of the themes of the *Inferno* is that we must accept the consequences of our own moral vision. Gogol surely intended to repeat this lesson here: Chichikov's morality is dubious. He needs to dupe other people in order to survive. In the first part of *Dead Souls*, he barely gets his comeuppance (although he is exposed as a cheat and a liar). It is thought that in the next two parts Gogol had planned, one way or another, he would have tortured Chichikov and sent him to hell. Similarly, a key message in Homer's *Odyssey* is the importance of loyalty to family. Chichikov has no family and no allegiances. He is a lonely and pathetic figure who belongs nowhere.

This is a novel about wealth, greed, hypocrisy and status. Chichikov wants to cheat the system by faking his wealth: the number of souls you owned indicated your fortune. Of course, you were not supposed to acquire large numbers of dead souls, but you were taxed according to how many serfs you originally owned. That number also conferred other advantages on you, offering the possibility of acquiring loans or mortgages. Gogol had happened upon the flaw in the system: what if someone never had any serfs but bought everyone else's dead ones? Couldn't that person end up richer than everyone else? And what sort of person would that make you? The answer: not a nice one.

Chichikov has all the clothes and all the patter of someone who deserves respect in Russian high society. The subservient, snobbish and self-serving characters he meets on his travels soon fall prey to his charms. But then he has a rapid reversal of fortune. Once he has acquired four hundred dead souls, Chichikov's plan is revealed as a cynical get-rich-quick scheme. He was intending to take out a loan against the souls and disappear with the money. He becomes a figure of hatred and suspicion, with some gossiping that he was going to elope with the governor's daughter and others speculating that Chichikov is, in fact, Napoleon in disguise. He flees to another part of Russia, where he masterminds a similar scheme, this time attempting to acquire an estate and forge a will, which results in his arrest. This was only Part 1 of a three-part novel, and it ends mid-sentence, with the prince who arrested him opining on this 'scandalous matter'. This is a book in which no one comes out of it looking good. Everyone is an anti-hero. It's a warning about life that's about as subtle as a burning cross: abandon hope all ye who enter this kind of moral universe.

In real life, Gogol was not a tedious, moralizing prig, however. Instead he was the most adorable of all the Russian writers because he was the greediest. He wasn't even hypocritical about it: he knew what he was like and freely admitted it. His biographers call his favourite pastime 'gourmandising'; I call it 'stuffing your face'. He was a man who loved to eat and suffered all his life with chronic indigestion, a lot of it caused by overindulgence. He wasn't necessarily the politest dinner guest. He loved rolling up bread into pellets and firing them at other people. And if he didn't like a drink, he would just pour it back into the decanter. He was a good host, though. He loved macaroni and had his own special recipe for it. And he liked to make punch. According to some accounts, he also claimed to be the inventor of a cocktail of boiled goat's milk and rum called Gogol Mogol. He didn't entirely invent it, however. From the seventeenth century onwards *kogel mogel* was a sort of Jewish eggnog with eggs, honey and milk, sometimes served as a cold remedy. Who can blame Gogol for wanting to own it himself, especially when it sounded as if it was named after him? (Apparently, Barbra Streisand's mother served her this drink as a child – without the rum, sadly – to strengthen her voice. It clearly worked.)

In photographs, Gogol does not look like you might expect. He can be a tiny bit porky-looking, but nothing excessive. He's actually quite good-looking, with a dashing pencil moustache and a sleek feminine bob. He was known for the attention he paid to his wardrobe, and he was the king of the frock coat. Still, all that food had an effect, and he died shortly before his forty-third birthday. All the overeating would have done nothing for his health. And yet when it came to it, in the end, he more or less starved himself and died in a state of utter misery. (And you thought Dostoevsky was a nightmare.)

Gogol was born in 1809 and died in 1852, at the age of forty-two. (All my favourites died young: Gogol, Bulgakov, Chekhov. The difficult ones – Solzhenitsyn and Tolstoy – just went on and on.) His work is seen as bridging the gap between Pushkin's idea of 'the first Russian novel' and the big classics of Dostoevsky and Tolstoy that came later. The language he uses in his books is seen as being 'simple Russian'. He, supposedly, had a 'poor knowledge' of Russian, which is a very odd thing to say about one of your country's greatest novelists. But all that is meant by this is that he doesn't use flowery language and classical references in his work. His novels are the stuff of the everyday, even in their titles: overcoats, noses, government inspectors. His books are not psychological studies or social commentaries (although, of course, under the surface they are both these things). They are about day-to-day life: offices, kitchens, hotels, streets, carriages. There is always a lesson about integrity: don't pretend to be something you're not, you'll get found out.

This quest for telling it like it is comes out in all Gogol's depictions of eating. It's almost as if he's so desperate not to be a hypocrite about his own greed that he overdoes it. From the beginning of *Dead Souls*, you can feel Gogol's obsession with fatness, thinness, hospitality, social eating and the business of feeding. Gogol is often referred to as being the master of the grotesque, and his fascination with food comes into this. But there is also something very joyous about him. He's like a snorty little pig sniffing out truffles, except the truffles are interesting (and, yes, sometimes gleefully grotesque) characters. There are no subtleties in his descriptions. The opening chapters describe how there are two types of men: fat and thin. The thin men lean into the ladies. The fat men know to stay away from the ladies. (Say what you like, but I can't help feeling that he has really got this right. Usually, the more portly someone is, the more aware they are of invading personal space. But if you are skinny and agile, you can get away with brushing up against others.) Don't pity the fat ones, though, because they are always the ones who come out on top in Gogol: 'The fat ones of this world know how to manage their affairs better than the thin ones.'

Chichikov is supposed to be a dreadful person, someone who eats three pancakes in a stack, rolled up and dipped in melted butter. The monster. But really, what's not to like about a man who wears a tailcoat of whortleberry-red hue shot through with a lighter weave? (Imagine the poor translator who had to get all that right. Whortleberry red? This jolly fruit is a sort of lingonberry, apparently. Heaven forbid Gogol should just say it's a scarlet or crimson jacket.) He covers up this delightful piece of attire with 'a greatcoat lined with bearskin'. That is some greatcoat. This is typical Gogol: detail, artifice, dandyism, fun. But always with a wink. Chichikov isn't really well dressed. He's wearing the emperor's new clothes. Gogol has a wonderful eye for detail and a lovely way of describing small moments. When Chichikov visits a landowner, the narrator takes it upon himself to describe the landowner's relationship with his wife: 'They would plant such a long and languorous kiss on each other that, for its duration, a small cheap cigar could easily have been smoked to the end.' Just as the greatcoat has got to be lined with no less than bearskin, that really does have to be an extremely long kiss. Gogol is not someone who likes to do things by halves. He is someone who is a consummate observer of others: their mannerisms, behaviour, speech patterns. These people are here because we need them for the story – and because they're funny. But they're also here to remind us that at least we're not as bad as everyone else.

Dead Souls is a highly effective cautionary tale about the perils of hypocrisy. Chichikov is a ridiculous character, but he is in many ways a likeable one. He's foppish and charmingly dressed. He is garrulous and has a turn of phrase that makes him seem attractive and entertaining at times. He has an irritatingly high regard for his own face and loves his chin so much that he strokes it as often as possible and likes to boast to his friends how perfectly round it is. (Hey, if I had a perfectly round chin, I would also do this.) He likes blowing his nose very loudly into a white handkerchief infused with eau de cologne, making a sound that is not unlike a trumpet blowing in your ear. This is described as being all rather fun and amusing. As readers, we need to see him this way because, otherwise, the book would not work: we wouldn't believe that the landowners would be deceived by his charm and hand over their dead souls. This is Gogol showing us what we should be really careful of. Hypocrites, con men and shysters are charismatic and damn good company.

Just before Chichikov realizes that he has now obtained almost four hundred souls, Gogol allows the narrator a digression that gives some insight into the message he was trying to impart with this work, which we have to suppose he would have fleshed out more fully if he had got to the end of the intended three parts. The narrator imagines a writer who is truly happy because he tells tales of heroic types who never put a foot wrong, who achieve fame far and wide and never descend to the depths of the ordinary life. But he is not this kind of writer, he adds. He is instead the sort who seeks to 'summon forth . . . all the dreadful, appalling morass of trifles that mire our lives . . .' This is the writer who shows the ugly truth and whom no one appreciates. Not for him the praise of his readers or the admiration of sixteen-year-old girl fans who will fly at him, 'head awhirl and hero-worshipful'. He continues to heap on the self-pity. This writer will never be acclaimed in his lifetime. The importance of the honesty of his work will never be understood. He will experience 'reproach' and 'ridicule'. This was true of Gogol, who received stern criticism in his time. 'Harsh is his chosen course,' the 'narrator' (i.e. Gogol himself) concludes, 'and bitterly will he feel his solitude.' Honesty is important and noble. But it will not necessarily make you liked.

What's cheering about *Dead Souls* is not only that Gogol is so funny, it's that you can tell he can't quite help loving the people he purports to hate, just a little bit. The novel is full of digressions designed to showcase the local characters Chichikov encounters on his travels, each one more ridiculous, pompous and self-deluded than the last. Could he show us any more clearly how we should *not* be behaving? One of my favourite portraits is that of the virtually comatose landowner Andrey Ivanovich Tentetnikov in Chapter 1 of Part 2, a character who has caused no end of headaches to translators. In one edition, he comes across as a romantic type: ' . . . he was not a bad person, he was simply a star-gazer'. But this isn't meant as a compliment. Other translations read differently: 'neither a good nor a bad being, but simply – a burner of the daylight' (Pevear and Volokhonsky translation). And this: 'a fellow crawling between earth and heaven' (Guerney and Fusso translation). All Gogol means is that this man is a layabout, a good-for-nothing, a lazybones, an idler. He makes this very clear by the end of the section: ' . . . Tentetnikov belonged to that species of people who are in no danger of becoming extinct in Russia, and who formerly bore such names as sluggards, lieabouts and couch-warmers'. These are exactly the people Gogol wants to skewer in this book. And yet, boy, does he make them seem amusing.

Things go badly for Tentetnikov after an altercation with the General, whose daughter he hoped to court. Tentetnikov gets fed up with the General referring to him in conversation as 'my friend' and 'my very dear fellow', as he thinks it's overfamiliar and patronizing. When the General finally uses *ty* instead of *vy* for 'you' to him (like *tu* and *vous* in French), Tentetnikov loses it completely and breaks off from the family. In the aftermath of this event, he becomes even more slothful and couch-warming than usual: 'His pantaloons even found their way into the parlour. On the elegant table in front of the sofa lay a pair of greasy braces, as if they had been set out as a refreshment for a guest.' (Only Gogol the gourmand could see a pair of braces on a table as looking like they'd been presented as a snack.) This is the moment when Chichikov enters the poor man's life, seeking someone new to scam. Tentetnikov becomes the catalyst for Chichikov's second adventure, when he convinces Chichikov to talk to the General on his behalf to repair relations between the two of them.

Tentetnikov, like dozens of other characters, is the embodiment of *poshlost'*, the fascinating Russian characteristic most closely associated with Gogol. Known as a virtually untranslatable word (and we all know how much I hate that idea), it means something like 'trashiness', 'tackiness', 'vulgarity', 'triviality'. It has a moral weight to it: once you have succumbed to *poshlost'* as an individual, your life is worthless. Nabokov defined it as 'the falsely important, the falsely beautiful, the falsely clever, the falsely attractive'. Sometimes, I wish Nabokov were still alive so that he could meet the Kardashians. The idea of hypocrisy is wrapped up in there, too. Gogol's job in *Dead Souls* is to show us that these people may believe themselves to be important and significant but, in fact, they are anything but. Someone who is *poshliy* (the adjective from the noun) doesn't know it; otherwise, they would stop themselves. Gogol evokes *poshlost'* at every turn, but he does it in such a way that you feel as though he loves these people, too. It's as if he can't quite bring himself to condemn them. Or perhaps it's just that he's brought these characters to life too vividly and so it's too easy to identify with them. (Or maybe I am just *poshlaya* and so I identify with the trash. This is very possible.)

Gogol had a bizarre childhood and perhaps an overly close relationship with his mother. She, at least, was a fervent supporter of his, although possibly too fervent. She believed him to be the best Russian author ever. Not an unreasonable thing if your son is a successful, published novelist. ('Pushkin who?') But she also believed that Gogol had invented the steamboat and the railway. It's good to have a supportive parent, but really. He hadn't even invented the Gogol Mogol, let alone the steamboat and the railway. One of Gogol's biographers, David Magarshack, writes, somewhat mournfully, I like to think: 'She pampered him as a child and was mainly responsible for his becoming a capricious egotist.' (Don't sit on the fence! Poor Gogol.)

Gogol is surely the most openly neurotic of all the Russian writers. He was fond of telling people that he had been to see a doctor in Paris who had told him that his stomach was upside down. This was a man for whom hypochondria became 'a way of life', as another biographer, Richard Peace, puts it. He almost enjoyed being ill, because it meant he could move from one European spa town to the next, always looking for some kind of self-improvement and never having to return to Russia. He often wrote to his friends about his ailments in great detail. From a letter in 1832: 'My health is exactly as it was when we met, except that my diarrhoea has stopped and I now have a tendency towards constipation.'

He did a lot of things towards the end of his life that made him very unpopular. When there was a gala performance of *The Government Inspector* in a theatre, he insisted on sitting on the floor in his box so that no one could see him. Presumably, from this position, he couldn't really see the play. When the curtain came down and people called for the author of the piece to take a bow, he crawled out of the box and ran out of the theatre and down the street. This was probably because of shyness and embarrassment, but when people heard what had happened they took it for immense arrogance.

He wrote a lot of unintentionally entertaining things in his letters from abroad: 'There is such a large number of vile faces in Russia, that I could not bear to look at them. Even now I feel like spitting when I remember them.' He can hardly be blamed for wanting to stay abroad for years at a time. He always seemed to find himself lovely friends, often ones who would lend him money, or at least take him out for excellent meals. In Baden Baden (where else?) at one point, he becomes friendly with a princess who makes a point of always serving him a special compote. (Not a euphemism.) The 'deceptions' of his later life were usually about the clash of his high living with his vows of asceticism. On the one hand, he wanted to party hard. On the other, he wanted to tell everyone that he was writing the world's greatest moral literary masterpiece and that he himself was a great moral and spiritual leader. He would write to his friends that he was living 'like a monk' and then go out for dinners that gave him the worst indigestion. It was around this time that he became obsessed with the aforementioned Barbra Streisand drink.

Peace gives a fantastic rundown of all his terrible qualities: 'his obsession with illness; his apparent asexuality; his flight from passion or from stagnation with constant travel; the strange treatment of his friends; his many deceptions . . .' (And this is a relatively sympathetic biographer.) The strange treatment of his friends refers to the latter part of his life, when Gogol started to follow a peculiar religious path which meant that nothing he could do was quite spiritual enough. And he began to force himself to renounce his previous works as 'sinful'. (Sound familiar? Hello, Tolstoy.) He took a great deal of pleasure in finding fault with himself as part of this spiritual quest and wrote endless letters to his friends, begging them to list all his deficiencies. He found this practice so fruitful that he began to write back to his friends, listing all their deficiencies in return, even though they had not asked him to do this. Oh, Gogol! In later life, he fell under the influence of a mystic who succeeded in convincing him that all his work was a sin. He burned most of Part 2 of *Dead Souls*, instantly regretted it and died nine days later, having refused all food.

I often wonder whether Gogol was just born a century too early. He was eccentric in a way that would have been regarded as odd in any era. (He once ordered a new wig as a treatment for writer's block, contradicting Solzhenitsyn's later statement that Russian writers never suffered from this problem. Gogol hoped the wig would 'open up the pores of [his] scalp'.) But a lot of his passions were connected to his sexuality: there is now a theory that he was almost certainly gay, at a time when he probably found it impossible to love another man, even privately. We don't know for certain. Intriguingly, there is a gap in his correspondence with one close friend, Danilevsky, that suggests that something happened between them. Maybe it was something wonderful but it just couldn't last. Or maybe it was a horrific moment when Gogol offended his friend in some way. We can't know. I do hope he knew some kind of love. He did later write that he really enjoyed playing billiards with Danilevsky and that the sound of billiard balls clacking together was one of the things in the world that made him happiest.

Gogol had something of a twentieth-century manner about him in the way that he saw the world, which is almost reminiscent of Salvador Dalí. In a letter from Rome in 1838, he wrote about the spring roses: 'I know you won't believe me, but I am often overcome by a mad desire to be turned into one enormous nose – to have nothing else, no eyes, no hands, no feet, except one huge nose with nostrils the size of large buckets so that I could inhale as much of the fragrance of spring as possible.' I hope, wherever he is, he is wearing a giant nose costume and playing billiards with his best friend.

What is satisfying about this theory of his sexuality is that it does explain a lot about Gogol: to our modern eyes, he seems to have been unnecessarily tortured. Dostoevsky's pains were very much ones that he brought on himself with his often terrible character, his gambling and his inability to face his demons (and, most likely, the not very advanced treatment of his epilepsy). Tolstoy's suffering was largely caused by his obsession with morality. Some of Gogol's suffering was self-inflicted, but I also have a lot of sympathy for the theory that he couldn't express his sexuality. This must have been torture for a man who considered a lack of hypocrisy as one of life's greatest virtues. He longed to impart this very modern lesson to others: be yourself, don't pretend to be something you're not, accept yourself for who you are – but he was unable to live it out himself.

11. How to Know What Matters in Life: *War and Peace* by Lev Tolstoy
(Or: Don't try to kill Napoleon)

'We thought it was the end of the world,
but it turned out for the best.'

After the shock of realizing that my Russian adventure had all been a sham, a fiction I had dreamed up in my own imagination to make myself feel more exotic or to feel like I belonged somewhere, I came to develop a more fluid attitude towards my identity. It doesn't have to be perfect, and it doesn't have to be fixed. It's not something that is gifted to you, whether by birth or by ancestry. It's not something you are. It's something you do. That's the most important lesson: it's all just a ride. You might as well enjoy the view and count your blessings.

And while Russia may not be a part of my blood heritage, it's a part of the life I have lived, and that can never be changed. Russian is not something that I will ever master, regardless of what my roots are, but it is something that can bring me great joy from the attempt at mastery alone. I will never give up on the language, and I will never give up on trying to understand these books. I never really needed to pretend to be Russian to get into them in the first place. That was just a story I told myself. I hope I would have found them anyway, in the way that any other normal person gravitates towards these books, because they are the ones that have stood the test of time. Now, I can enjoy them like any other reader, instead of having the pressure of thinking, 'Ah, yes, these are my people . . .' Which they never were in the first place.

I approached a re-reading of *War and Peace* from this new perspective of embracing imperfection. One of the most important things about the novel for anyone who hasn't read it, and also for anyone who has tried to read it and supposedly 'failed', is to understand that to read this novel is not a one-off task. Reading it is the work of a lifetime. There's no such thing as 'failing' to read *War and Peace*. You just haven't got enough practice in yet. It's essential to regard it rather like riding a bicycle. There will be a first time, when you wonder how anyone can ride a bicycle at all. There will be times when you ride the bicycle frequently and it seems like second nature. Maybe you will even feel like you are in the Tour de France. And there will be times when your bicycle-riding is so rusty that you wonder if it's worth bothering with because you will probably cause an accident, resulting in physical damage, if not to yourself, then to others. The key is to keep getting back on the bicycle.

The reason this relaxed approach is so important is that *War and Peace*, perhaps more than any novel, has come to represent 'Russian literature'. So the person who puts himself or herself off it for whatever reason (by insisting on a perfect, flawless reading experience, for example) risks putting themselves off not only Tolstoy's work but the whole of Russian literature. Don't think of *War and Peace* as a novel. Think of it as the Bible. You wouldn't expect to sit down and read the Bible cover to cover, would you? And if there were bits of the Bible you found boring, you wouldn't let it put you off reading it for ever, would you? And yet this is what people do all the time with *War and Peace*. (In fact, you might easily get put off reading the Bible. That comparison has collapsed rather too easily. Forget I said the Bible. It's not like the Bible. It's like a lot of novels mushed together.)

It has taken me years to realize all this. I didn't read *War and Peace* properly (really properly) until I knew it was going to be on television. Of all the Russian books, it is the most daunting, the most intimidating and the most full of pages. So many pages. Despite my own passionately held belief that no one should ever be put off by any book ever, this one put me off for a long time. A first attempt suggested to me that there was just too much skirmishing. Seriously. The word 'skirmish' is on virtually every page. Plus, there are over five hundred characters. It's meandering and, at times, confusing. Henry James categorized the classic novels of the nineteenth century as 'large, loose, baggy monsters'. And *War and Peace* is the largest and the loosest and the baggiest monster of them all. James also called it 'a fluid pudding'. In short, it is a bloated, blubbery Godzilla of a blancmange.

And yet. Isn't the whole of life a wobbly Godzilla jelly? Isn't life full of non sequiturs, unlikely coincidences, hundreds of characters who may or may not be significant? So much so that it could be argued that the structure of *War and Peace* is one of the most honest reflections of real life in literature. It's sequential and chronological. It's sometimes uneventful for ages and then suddenly far more eventful than you would like. Not everything that happens makes sense. There are many digressions. There are many surprises. There are few happy endings, and even the endings that are happy are complicated and hard-won. But if you can stick with it and sit through the dull bits and find people to champion and elements that you're passionate about, it is a strange and wonderful thing. (You see? I could be talking about *War and Peace*. Or I could be talking about life. So clever. Not me. Tolstoy.)

The great challenge of *War and Peace* is not only to extract the lessons from the stories and characters in the novel – enjoy every sunrise and sunset; know who your friends are; beware the folly of youth; have faith in your own future; be kind and humble – it's to find the lesson about yourself as a reader which is revealed in how you tackle the process of reading it. Again, like life itself, it seems insurmountable. Sometimes, it seems pointless. Other times, it makes no sense at all. And yet, if you can be patient and kind to yourself, it will slowly open up to you. The trick is to go at it at your own pace and patiently let it go when it's not working. You can always return to it. The novelist Philip Hensher, who has written beautifully of his intense lifelong love for *War and Peace*, suggests that, when you're really into it, it can be read in ten days. I think this is realistic. But it does depend on being really into it. And that is not always easy.

War and Peace started out as a novel called 'The Decembrists' and, at one point, Tolstoy considered calling it 'All's Well That Ends Well'. (I know *War and Peace* is not the most imaginative title. But, really. It could have been a lot worse.) He began the novel in 1863, a year after his marriage to Sofya Andreyevna. It was written over six years, at, arguably, one of the happiest times of Tolstoy's life. The four children born during this period all lived to a ripe old age. This was a very different man to the one who wrote *Anna Karenina*. The year he started that novel, they lost a child for the first time. Two more babies died over the next three years. I don't want to make too much of this, as I know that in the olden days infant mortality was more common than it is nowadays. But it doesn't seem outlandish to suggest that a man who was already deeply moved by life and its injustices could be profoundly affected by the death of three children in a row. No wonder, by the time he had finished writing *Anna Karenina*, he had a growing obsession with religion and death and had written of his desire to commit suicide. During the writing of *War and Peace*, though, which is the purest expression of Tolstoy's most positive philosophies of life, all this was yet to come.

I'm not sure it's wise for anyone to attempt a synopsis of *War and Peace*. But we've come this far and, in the circumstances, it seems rude not to. The novel opens in the salons of St Petersburg in 1805, where the talk is of an impending war with France. Pierre Bezukhov, the son of a dying count, is finding it hard to integrate into high society, having returned from his education abroad. He is disillusioned. He finds everyone pretentious. His friend Prince Andrei Bolkonsky is married to pregnant society beauty Liza. He is also disillusioned. And he finds his wife pretentious. Prince Andrei is soon to head off for war, leaving his lightly but attractively mustachioed wife with his grumpy father and religious-fanatic sister, Maria.

Meanwhile, in Moscow, the Rostov family, typically for some aristocrats of the time, have overstretched themselves financially and hope desperately for salvation through the marriage of one of their four children, ideally their son Nikolai, who is about to join the army. Their daughter Natasha is in love with Boris Drubetskoy, who is also about to join the army. Inconveniently, Sonya, an orphaned cousin raised by the family, is in love with Nikolai. He loves her back, which is bad because she has no dowry. Poor Sonya.

Nikolai goes off to war and comes back with the dashing officer Denisov, who proposes to Natasha and is rebuffed. Pierre's father dies and, suddenly, Pierre is a wealthy heir and the toast of society. He is persuaded into marrying Hélène, the bitchy and corrupt (but very beautiful) daughter of Prince Kuragin. Dolokhov (a friend of Denisov) is one of Hélène's lovers, and Pierre duels with him, with Dolokhov ending up wounded. Pierre is traumatized by this incident and disappears off to travel and join the Freemasons. (I know. Don't overthink it.)

Prince Andrei returns from war to find his wife dying in childbirth. Now, he and Pierre are both feeling guilty at having caused the suffering of others. Andrei recovers sufficiently to travel to St Petersburg to further his military career and there, at a ball, he meets Natasha and they fall in love. Prince Andrei's grumpy father opposes the match, asking them to wait a year before marrying. Prince Andrei goes abroad to have his war wounds treated.

While he's away, Natasha goes to Moscow and meets Hélène and her creepy brother Anatole. The two siblings conspire to imperil Natasha's honour, and she is seduced by Anatole, agreeing to elope with him. She breaks off her engagement to Andrei. But their plans to elope are uncovered and Natasha is disgraced. She tries to commit suicide. Andrei returns and refuses to propose to her again. Pierre attempts to persuade him but realizes that he has fallen in love with Natasha himself. The great comet of 1812 is seen in the sky, considered a portentous sign of the invasion by Napoleon.

The little Frenchman is indeed advancing by this point, and Pierre becomes obsessed with the idea that he, Pierre, must kill Napoleon. (This is a really bad idea, as Pierre has no military knowledge or physical strength. Also, he is fairly inept.) Maria tends to her dying father and is left as mistress of the family's country seat. Nikolai Rostov is among the troops passing through Maria's district. The two meet and fall in love. Pierre goes to the front and flounders around, distressed by the useless slaughter. Prince Andrei is also at the front. When he is wounded by a shell, he finds himself in the operating theatre next to Anatole Kuragin, who is having his leg amputated.

Natasha sets up her home as a station for wounded soldiers. Prince Andrei is one of the soldiers sent there. Natasha nurses him. By this point, Prince Andrei must be afraid to close his eyes as, every time he opens them, someone from his past is on the bed next to him. Anyway, he dies, but not before forgiving Natasha. Napoleon enters Moscow. Pierre continues to attempt various heroics, at one point saving a child from a fire. Hélène dies, probably from some kind of abortion-causing medicine. Nikolai thinks about marrying Maria. He receives a letter from Sonya, releasing him from any understanding. It's a letter Sonya has been forced to write by Nikolai's mother (who still hopes he will marry into money). Pierre is captured by the French. He meets the prisoner Platon Karatayev, who tells him the meaning of life.

Napoleon makes some crucial errors and has to abandon Moscow, while the Russians allow the French to retreat. Dolokhov and Denisov attack the fleeing French and free Pierre. Natasha and Pierre are reunited and, eventually, decide to marry. Nikolai marries Maria. There is some musing about the existence of bees in the epilogue, and Tolstoy concludes that free will is an illusion. He goes on a bit about Copernicus and Newton and Voltaire. That's it. *War and Peace* aficionados will note that I have not mentioned much about General Kutuzov, Count Rostopchin or the Battle of Borodino. All I can say in my defence is that we all find our ways of getting through this novel, and let's not judge.

One of the things that fascinates me most about *War and Peace* is Tolstoy's ability to construct these concentric relationship circles and make them seem believable. Just as in *Anna Karenina*, where Anna and Vronsky can be together only because Kitty and Vronsky do *not* end up together (and so then Kitty can end up with Levin), so, in *War and Peace*, the relationship between Andrei and Natasha is doomed in order for Natasha to go off with Pierre. Similarly, Sonya needs to be dispatched to allow Maria and Nikolai their happiness. Even a minor character like Denisov suffers this 'domino effect' fate: his marriage proposal to Natasha is rejected, only for him to be instrumental in Pierre's rescue later on, so that Pierre can survive and . . . marry Natasha.

This is a frequent lesson of Tolstoy's: sometimes our

unhappiness facilitates someone else's happiness. It's all meant to happen for a reason. And it is all being guided by a hand which has far more power over us than our own hopes and desires. That hand seems, in the end, to be relatively benign: despite all the suffering and misery that have been endured, there is happiness and stability at the end, and a joy in a quiet, hard-won family love that seemed out of reach to both Natasha and Pierre at many points during the novel. We don't all get what we deserve. But we get what we get and, by accepting it, sometimes it can make us happier than we were expecting to be. Again, it's a simple lesson: count your blessings.

What about fate? Fate is everywhere here, of course. So much so that the role of coincidence in *War and Peace* makes *Doctor Zhivago* look almost like an accurate historical record. When Dolokhov attacks a French regiment, it just happens to be the regiment holding Pierre prisoner. What are the odds? Of all the places Prince Andrei could end up in his convalescence . . . it has to be Natasha's home. But Tolstoy gets away with it by spreading out the coincidences across many, many pages so that you don't really notice them until you get to the end and look back. But we experience many incredible coincidences and bizarre outcomes in life that would never seem likely enough to use in fiction. And there would be no narrative without the interweaving of these characters who need to interact with each other across fifteen years and a huge geographical landscape. Nonetheless, it does seem a remarkable leap of faith to suggest that, if you went off to war with hundreds of thousands of other soldiers, you would end up bumping into one of your childhood chums . . . But who are we to criticize?

Setting aside this rich and strangely realistic narrative, Tolstoy's entire philosophy can be summed up in one scene, in the time it takes for Pierre to eat a baked potato with a sprinkling of salt on it. This episode is the heart and soul of the book and can be read in five minutes: Volume 4, Part 1, Chapter 12 (page 1,074 in the Penguin Classics edition mentioned in the Recommended Reading list). It encapsulates the message of this book and of Tolstoy's life overall. Of all the characters who represent Tolstoy in his own work – Levin in *Anna Karenina*, Pierre in *War and Peace* – the one who speaks the most for the author is the prisoner Platon Karatayev, the offerer of the salty potato, who appears fleetingly over the course of these five pages. Pierre meets him when they have both been captured by the French. Karatayev is a proper Russian *muzhik* (peasant): plain-talking, wise, the very salt of the earth. He imparts several lessons to Pierre, which take on a profound significance in the context of Tolstoy's life long after the publication of *War and Peace* and, later, *Anna Karenina*.

Karatayev's life lessons are simple. Be grateful for the relationship you have with your mother. (Tolstoy's mother died when he was two.) Make sure you enjoy family life. (His father died when he was nine.) Be sure to have children of your own. (He had thirteen, eight of whom survived infancy.) If you have your own house or family estate, know that you are lucky. (Tolstoy inherited the family estate at Yasnaya Polyana in 1847, at the age of nineteen.) Put salt on your potatoes and enjoy them as if they are a special treat. (Tolstoy became an obsessive vegetarian later in life.)

Karatayev adds: 'The great thing is to get on with other people.' Tolstoy followed this advice only occasionally, in my view, and certainly not at the moment when he was telling Chekhov that his plays were worse than Shakespeare's. But we can't all follow our own advice, can we? The most important things are stoicism and resignation: 'The beggar's bowl or the prison hole, you have to take what comes.' Bearing in mind that Tolstoy is aware that Pierre is the character most close to him personally, he allows Pierre to take Karatayev's words to heart: ' . . . Platon Karatayev would always stay in his mind as a most vivid and precious memory, the epitome of kind-heartedness and all things rounded and Russian.'

If only we could all be like Platon Karatayev. He is described as being over fifty but looking much younger than his years. He has 'strong, white teeth' which show whenever he laughs, which is often. (Surely wishful thinking in nineteenth-century Russia? Both the whiteness of the teeth and the frequency of the laughter.) He loves to sing when evening comes. And whenever he wakes up, he's straight out of bed, giving himself a shake-down and getting on with it. Come to think of it, I imagine Platon Karatayev might have been an extremely annoying person, especially first thing in the morning. But let's overlook that.

There's even an echo of the famous *Anna Karenina* epigraph ('Vengeance is mine. And I will repay.') in the old man's ramblings. 'Fate picks you out. And 'ere we be, always passing judgement – that's not right, doesn't suit us.' It is not for human beings to pass judgement or exact vengeance. That is God's work. We must bear our fate with acceptance and patience. 'Our 'appiness, me dear, be like water in a drag-net. Swells out lovely when you pulls; take it out and it's empty.' Karatayev's great strength is his spontaneity and the fact that he is not hung up on words and their meanings: he says what he likes, when he feels like it. He is the definition of someone who is natural and at peace with himself. 'Words and actions flowed from him as smoothly, inevitably and spontaneously as fragrance from a flower.' If we can learn anything, then it's this: ' . . . he loved and showed affection to every creature he came across in life, especially people, no particular people, just those who happened to be there before his eyes.' This is the person Tolstoy tried to become when he gave up his 'frivolous' novels. It represents the setting aside of the multifaceted fox who is interested in everyone and everything in favour of the hedgehog, one with all its prickles removed, sitting chanting a Buddhist mantra. It's great life advice, if only anyone could actually follow it.

I feel lucky that I came to *War and Peace* at a time when I was no longer obsessed with trying to be Russian or even conflicted about the fact that I had spent such a long time trying to be Russian and had turned out to be something different. The further I moved away from trying to be Russian, the closer I came to being myself: someone from a simple yet complicated background who had tried to fill in the gaps with a bit of imagination. Maybe too much imagination. By the time I came to *War and Peace* as a grown-up who knew who she was, not as a child wishing she were someone else, I had made peace with that story. That is almost certainly the best way to approach it. Which is not to say that you shouldn't read *War and Peace* when you are younger. Perhaps many people can. But I really struggled to appreciate it when I dipped into it as a student, my eyes glazing over as I flipped the pages through the 'War' bits. It was something I needed to read when I had some idea of my own story and my own thoughts about how life unfolds.

The novelist Ann Patchett has summed up the joy of Russian literature expertly: it's not so much about reading it as about re-reading it. She describes reading *Anna Karenina* at the age of twenty-one and believing that Anna and Vronsky were the most charming, romantic people in the world and that Kitty and Levin the most boring, pathetic people in the world. She writes, 'Last year I turned 49, and I read the book again. This time, I loved Levin and Kitty . . . Anna and Vronsky bored me.' As we get older, she concludes, 'we gravitate towards the quieter, kinder plotlines, and find them to be richer than we had originally understood them to be'. *War and Peace* echoed the plotline of my own life: lots of bits that I didn't want to look at or know about; lots of bits I didn't understand until I had children of my own; lots of bits that only made sense once I had realized that life does not have to be exciting and dynamic in order to be interesting. What matters more is this quieter kindness that Patchett mentions.

This is the key to tackling *War and Peace*: personalize it. What do you want to get out of it? Why are you reading it? How can you mould your reading of it to your own personal tastes and habits? Not to belabour the point but, again, it's just like life: what do you want from this experience? Andrew Davies, the screenwriter who adapted the novel for the television series that took me back to the book, was realistic about his task. He got a second-hand paperback copy of the novel, picked up a pair of scissors and cut it up into chunks. If this is what it takes for you to carry it around with you, I do not think this is a terrible thing to do. Tolstoy would rather you read it than didn't read it, I suspect. And he won't mind if you buy an extra second-hand copy to cut up. (Although do buy a new copy, too. We want to keep his estate thriving.)

The other trick is to imagine it as several novels and a short story at the end (the epilogue). Whatever gets you through it. I like to read it three or four chapters at a time. I also like to choose a particular family or character to champion at different points. Usually, Pierre's perspective keeps me going (there's never that long a wait to get back to Pierre's story). Or you can follow it from the point of view of one of five families: the Bezukhovs, the Bolkonskys, the Rostovs, the Kuragins, the Drubetskoys. *War and Peace* is not the same as *Anna Karenina* at all (which is sort of *War and Peace* but only about the families), but it was the prototype for *Anna Karenina* in many ways. So if you have to fool yourself by thinking, 'It's okay. It's just like reading *Anna Karenina*,' then so be it. You are not that far off the mark. If you really want to give yourself an easy time (and I fully recommend it), the Penguin Classics edition in Recommended Reading has a chapter-by-chapter synopsis, one line at a time over sixteen and a half pages. In theory, you can use that and say you've read *War and Peace* in half an hour. In reality, it's a very useful reference guide to help you keep your bearings through the novel. And a great resource to use when re-reading it and wanting to find specific passages or tackle anew bits that you found challenging before.

There's something deeply reassuring in the relentless nature of Tolstoy's own search for happiness. This was a man who was known at university as 'Lyovochka the bear', because he was so bad-tempered. But we can see from the outside that he led a full and fulfilled life: a long marriage, a big family, an extraordinary literary legacy and a legion of followers for his spiritual philosophy. Yet he lived with such honesty and integrity he could not help but admit that for much of his life he was tortured by his own inadequacies and his inability to come to terms with life's injustices. In spite of the pain of this, he never gave up trying. One of the defining moments of his life had come at the age of five, when his beloved brother Nikolai told him he had found the secret to life and inscribed it on a green stick which he had buried in the ground. When this stick was uncovered and the secret known, it would put an end to all death and all wars. Tolstoy took this extremely seriously and spent his life meditating on that stick and trying to find it, both literally and metaphorically. When he was buried at his estate at Yasnaya Polyana, it was on the patch of ground where Nikolai was supposed to have buried the stick. He never did find out what was written on it. Although, in a way, he never needed to, as he wrote everything that the stick could have had written on it in his novels.

Perhaps Tolstoy had all kinds of reasons for struggling to find peace of mind. He might also have had his own secrets we can never know about. The character of Natasha in *War and Peace* is said to be based not on Sofya Andreyevna, his wife, but on her younger sister Tanya (who almost married one of Tolstoy's brothers). Given that Natasha is representative of idealized womanhood (in a way that Anna Karenina cannot be said to be), that might have been a very uncomfortable fact for Sofya. Tanya, like Natasha, could perform Russian dances, had a beautiful, clear singing voice and loved attending balls. According to one account, Tanya once told Tolstoy she was concerned she was outstaying her welcome with the family. He told her not to worry, she was earning her keep by 'posing for her portrait'. He was observing her in order to create a fictional character out of her. There's no suggestion of anything more than this, yet I can't help but think about Sofya Andreyevna transcribing that novel by hand, knowing that the main female character was based not on her but on her sister. Similarly, according to Aylmer Maude's biography, Sofya had herself written a short novel – which she destroyed – that supposedly held the inspiration for Natasha Rostova's relationship with her mother in *War and Peace*. Those two facts must be extremely annoying when you are copying out someone else's novel seven times and you discover that a) the heroine is very much like your younger sister and b) a major relationship in the novel is very similar to something you wrote. But I'm speculating here.

All this detail is unimportant when it comes to understanding *War and Peace* in theory. But for me it's been crucial in humanizing the author of a book with such a gargantuan reputation. It's a case of separating the genius from the man. Recognizing the gap between Tolstoy's wishful thinking about the perfect life and the reality of the life he actually led has been a huge comfort. *Anna Karenina* was what gave me my first addictive fix of Russianness, reeled me in and left me hooked on romantic, big ideas that allowed me to escape the confines of childhood and a family who didn't seem to want to know much about their identity. Over time, all of that unravelled and proved to be as much of a fiction as any Russian novel. And yet, as I came to *War and Peace* in later life, with children of my own and a whole other family that I have built for myself, I found a way for these stories and philosophies to 'fix' me as a person, both in the sense of mending me (because it's always comforting to know that other human beings are just as messed up as you are, even Tolstoy) and in the sense of 'fixing' or 'stabilizing' my identity. I will never be a beautiful and dramatic woman (although I seem to have unwittingly cultivated an upper-lip moustache which would have driven Tolstoy wild with desire). I will not attract the attention of a handsome, dark stranger in a flurry of snowflakes at the station. I am not and will never be Russian. But I am comfortable in my identity as someone who will always love stories and find solace in them.

My own life moved further away from Russia the more I became enmeshed in family life. I also realized that in focusing so heavily on the identity I felt had been denied to me, I'd turned away from looking at the things I was really drawn to in life. After that email from my unknown uncle in Canada, things were settled, even if they had been resolved in a way that made me feel small. I had been stupid for wanting to be different, for wanting to 'prove' something about my roots. I had become addicted to chasing a dream. Giving up on it was sobering. I preferred it when I could say, 'I don't know where my name comes from. But there's no reason why I couldn't be Russian . . .' So the lesson in *War and Peace* is apt: what matters in life is being comfortable with what you have and who you are.

Meanwhile, my extremely English husband made it his business to track down all the information he could about my ancestors. Whether this was motivated by his own curiosity to know the truth or out of empathy for me, I don't know. I think a bit of both. The strange thing is, I would never have gone after all the official records and census documents that he went after. I had had enough of knowing. I knew my uncle had not got it wrong. It had been confirmed by too many people. And so that was that. I had very little desire to find out any more. My fantasy had been exposed and I wanted to forget the whole thing.

Over the next few years, though, Simon collected the facts. According to the census, Gershon Groskop came to Stockton-on-Tees in 1861. His father was called Ashkel. And to one of his sons Gershon gave the name Levi, which means 'joined' or 'attached' in Hebrew. (I still marvel that the word 'Jewish' was not uttered once during my childhood.) Levi was my great-grandfather. He died a few years before I was born. My father knew him as a child. I will probably never know what made Gershon leave Łódź, why he chose England and not another destination and why, when he arrived, he pretty much stopped being Jewish immediately: he married a young Englishwoman, cutting out the female line. We don't know what he was running away from or running towards in the 1860s. He left a place with a population of around 15,000 that swelled to 500,000 before the Second World War, of whom around 200,000 were Jewish. When the Soviet army liberated Łódź from the Nazis in 1945, only 877 Jews were left alive. Maybe none of Gershon's descendants were involved in all that. Maybe they had all already gone abroad by then, just as he had. But it's something I think about.

In England, he cannot have had an easy life as an immigrant: he was a rag-and-bone man when he first came over here. The respectability of selling things did become a family trait and informed my grandfather's pride about owning his own shop. I have a picture from the late nineteenth century of some of my relatives selling nougat from a market stall. I often wonder whether Levi would have spoken any Yiddish to my grandfather when he was a child. My grandfather seemed to have no knowledge of such things, although my grandma used to say she could remember her father-in-law, Levi, muttering to himself in a strange language and wearing a skullcap. I don't know if that was fanciful on her part or something that she realized only once the obvious truth had been spoken out loud. Certainly, no one talked about these things before the email from the Canadian uncle. In the light of my enthusiastic but pointless quest for an identity, 'Groskop' itself turned out to be an extraordinary example of nominative determinism. A friend who speaks Yiddish later told me that Groskop ('big head') could mean many things: arrogant, big-headed, large of brain, intellectual. Or it could just mean stupid. My full name translates as 'Lively Fathead'. Oh, the irony.

A long time after all this, I figured out another piece of the puzzle. I knew I'd been attracted to Russian through the literature and through my weird name. But I had always wondered why it had to be Russian. Why had I tuned into that? Where did it come from? There was no reason for me to pick up a copy of *Anna Karenina*, in particular. There was no real reason for any of it. Why hadn't I decided my name was Dutch and become interested in, say, Rembrandt, and tried to become a painter? (This would have made about as much sense as what I did do.) Much later, in a conversation with my father, I realized that my grandparents had a Russian woman as a next-door neighbour when they had been living in the grocery store they ran when I was a child. This woman – I couldn't picture her – would most likely have been one of the first customers for the peg dolls I used to sell for five pence, sitting on top of the shop counter. She must have had an accent. She must have been unusual. She would have stuck in my mind. And I would have asked where she was from. And she would have said: 'Russia.'

This was the place where I had gone to live shortly after my sister was born. I was three years old and away from my parents for the first time. My most striking memories of my childhood are of this time. I would not have known anyone 'foreign' until that moment, and I did not meet a single other Russian person apart from this woman until I went to university and was taught

Russian. I can't know for sure, but I think something about her nudged something in me. Or a memory of her sparked something off when I read something . . . I can't know. If I ever had a memory of her, it has gone. But she is the only connection in my past to Russia, and the one I formed in my subconscious. It must all go back to her.

The funny thing is, I later discovered that there is a wonderful blurring of origin in all the documents relating to Gershon Groskop. I don't imagine he would have been literate or particularly able to speak much English. All the census documents carry his replies to the question of where he comes from. It will have been noted down by another person, so I have to wonder whether they prompted him or changed what he said to something they could understand. But he never says: 'Łódź, Poland.' Because he would not have thought of that as being where he came from: Poland did not regain its independence until 1918. I imagine his identity would have been Jewish and his language would have been Yiddish. But here – astonishingly, in black and white on the official documents – is what Gershon liked to answer when he told people where he was from: 'Russia', 'Prussia' and 'Prussian Russia'. He was never, strictly, Russian, and neither, strictly, am I. But the territory we come from formed part of the Russian empire. So, even though I was wrong, I was right after all. Prussia is close enough. Now all I need to do is grow some thicker eyelashes and I'll virtually be Anna Karenina after all.

Of course, I realize now that none of this matters. It's good to know where you come from in the past, but it's more important to know who you are right now. And the two are not the same. Gershon and I have somehow come full circle. He clearly decided – probably subconsciously – that if he was going to start a new life, he was going to let go of his old identity and be British. There was no need to mention that he was Jewish. Within a few generations, it had become the truth. I went the opposite way, trying to erase his attempts to assimilate. We were both just trying to make life easier for ourselves – and more meaningful. Isn't that what everyone tries to do? He wanted to belong somewhere. So did I. My truth was no better – and no worse – than his. Neither of us had it quite right. He wasn't British, and I'm not Russian. We can meet in the middle. Because we are all a sum of the people we come from. And yet we're also nothing to do with them. Much more than our history, we are an expression of the things we have seen, the books we have read, the people we have known and loved in this lifetime. Tolstoy knew this better than anyone, and it was the one truth he championed with the same passion he reserved for his occasional slice of lemon tart. 'Everything that I understand,' he wrote, 'I understand only because I love.'

Recommended Reading

This reading list details all the translated texts I worked from and gives a summary of many of the secondary sources I drew on. Anything I mention here is included because I recommend it. One book in particular forms the backdrop to this whole project. It is an essential read for anyone who loves the Russian classics: Elif Batuman's *The Possessed: Adventures with Russian Books and the People Who Read Them* (Granta, 2012). I interviewed Elif Batuman for the *Daily Telegraph* in 2011, and it was that conversation which galvanized me to develop the ideas in this book, which had been brewing since I took my undergraduate degree in Russian in 1995. For wonderful background on Russian fiction in translation, I must recommend David Remnick's legendary 2005 *New Yorker* essay 'The Translation Wars', which explains why the best translators see their work as similar to the restoration of great paintings, why Tolstoy was better paid than Dostoevsky and why the words 'f★★★ing bastards' should not appear in *War and Peace*.

Introduction

The edition of Lev Tolstoy's *A Calendar of Wisdom* referred to is the 2015 Alma Classics paperback, translated by Roger Cockrell.

1. *How to Know Who You Really Are:* Anna Karenina *by Lev Tolstoy*

I've worked from the 2000 Penguin Classics edition, translated by Richard Pevear and Larissa Volokhonsky, although I also make reference to the first edition of *Anna Karenina* I ever read, Rosemary Edmonds's 1978 translation, also Penguin Classics. (This is the one with Kramskoi's *Portrait of an Unknown Woman* on the cover.). See also *A Confession* by Lev Tolstoy from the Penguin Books Great Ideas series (2008), translated by Jane Kentish. This chapter – and the idea for this book – was inspired partly by Pavel Basinsky's wonderful biography *Leo Tolstoy: Flight from Paradise* (Glagoslav, 2015), translated by Huw Davies and Scott Moss. A friend gave me a copy of the book in Russian when it first came out in 2010. I was then lucky enough to interview Pavel Basinsky at the London Book Fair in 2014 for the PEN Literary Salon. I've also drawn on some of the stories and anecdotes A. N. Wilson recounts in his excellent biography *Tolstoy* (Atlantic Books, 2012) and on Henri Troyat's biography *Tolstoy* (Penguin, 1970), translated by Nancy Amphoux.

2. *How to Face Up to Whatever Life Throws at You:* Doctor Zhivago *by Boris Pasternak*

I used the 2002 Vintage edition of *Doctor Zhivago*, translated by Max Hayward and Manya Harari. *A Captive of Time: My Years with Pasternak – The Memoirs of Olga Ivinskaya* (Collins and Harvill Press, 1978), translated by Max Hayward, was hugely useful for background.

3. How to be Optimistic in the Face of Despair: Requiem *by Anna Akhmatova*

I worked from *The Complete Poems of Anna Akhmatova* (Canongate, 2000), edited with an introduction by Roberta Reeder and translated by Judith Hemschemeyer. This is a spectacular edition of Akhmatova. I also recommend *Twentieth-century Russian Poetry* (Fourth Estate, 1993), edited by Albert C. Todd and Max Hayward (with Daniel Weissbort), foreword by Yevgeny Yevtushenko, for an excellent introduction to Russian poetry in general.

I am a bit of an Akhmatova geek (I wrote my undergraduate dissertation on 'Poem Without a Hero') and so I recommend a lot here: *The Guest from the Future: Anna Akhmatova and Isaiah Berlin* by György Dalos (Farrar, Straus and Giroux, 1999), translated by Antony Wood; *Anna Akhmatova: Poet and Prophet* by Roberta Reeder (St Martin's Press, 1994); *Anna of All the Russias: The Life of Anna Akhmatova* by Elaine Feinstein (Vintage Books USA, 2007); *Remembering Anna Akhmatova* by Anatoly Nayman (Henry Holt & Co., 1993), translated by Wendy Rosslyn; *Anna Akhmatova: A Poetic Pilgrimage* by Amanda Haight (Oxford University Press, 1990); and *The Akhmatova Journals* by Lydia Chukovskaya (HarperCollins, 1994). I also found Nadezhda Mandelstam's *Hope against Hope* (Harvill Press, 1971), translated by Max Hayward, hugely helpful for background.

4. How to Survive Unrequited Love: A Month in the Country *by Ivan Turgenev*

I used a very easily available (and cheap) edition of *A Month in the Country: A Comedy in Five Acts*, the one from CreateSpace

Independent Publishing Platform (2015). It's the Constance Garnett translation. I've drawn on material from the 2000 Bloomsbury edition of Turgenev's *Letters*, edited and translated by A. V. Knowles. I've also used anecdotes from Avrahm Yarmolinsky's *Turgenev: The Man, His Art and His Age* (Orion Press, 1959); Robert Dessaix's beautiful travelogue *Twilight of Love: Travels with Turgenev* (Scribner, 2005); and *Turgenev: A Life* by David Magarshack (Faber and Faber, 1954).

5. How to Not be Your Own Worst Enemy: Eugene Onegin *by Alexander Pushkin*

I worked from the 2003 Penguin classics edition of *Eugene Onegin*, translated by Charles Johnston. Very few books have given me as much pleasure and as many laughs as *The Feud: Vladimir Nabokov, Edmund Wilson and the End of a Beautiful Friendship* by Alex Beam (Pantheon, 2016). For more on the background to the relationship between Wilson and Nabokov, see *Dear Bunny, Dear Volodya: The Nabokov–Wilson Letters, 1940–1971* (University of California Press, 2001), edited by Simon Karlinsky.

6. How to Overcome Inner Conflict: Crime and Punishment *by Fyodor Dostoevsky*

I worked from the 1993 Vintage edition of *Crime and Punishment*, translated by Richard Pevear and Larissa Volokhonsky. Isaiah Berlin's essay 'The Hedgehog and the Fox' is in his collection *Russian Thinkers* (Hogarth Press, 1978), which also has useful chapters on Turgenev and Tolstoy. I heartily recommend Ronald Hingley's biography *Dostoyevsky: His Life and Work* (Charles Scribner's Sons, 1978). Also useful: *Dostoevsky and the*

Woman Question by Nina Pelikan Straus (Palgrave Macmillan, 1994); *Dostoevsky's Greatest Characters: A New Approach to 'Notes from the Underground'*, Crime and Punishment *and* The Brothers Karamazov by Bernard J. Paris (Palgrave Macmillan, 2008); and *Dostoevsky: Works and Days* by Avrahm Yarmolinsky (Funk and Wagnalls, 1971).

7. How to Live with the Feeling that the Grass is Always Greener: Three Sisters *by Anton Chekhov*

I worked from a 2008 Digireads edition of *Three Sisters*, translated by Julius West. I love Rosamund Bartlett's *Chekhov: Scenes from a Life* (Simon & Schuster, 2004) and have drawn on a number of details she mentions. Virginia Woolf's essay 'The Russian Point of View' is in *The Common Reader*, Vol. 1 (Vintage, 2003) and is truly fascinating.

8. How to Keep Going When Things Go Wrong: One Day in the Life of Ivan Denisovich *by Alexander Solzhenitsyn*

I used the 2000 Penguin Classics edition, translated by Ralph Parker. A number of interviews and articles were helpful, including David Remnick's *New Yorker* pieces ('The Exile Returns' from 1994 and 'Deep in the Woods' from 2001), Andrew Higgins's 1994 interview with Natalia Reshetovskaya in the *Independent* and Vitali Vitaliev's 2000 report from Vermont for the *Daily Telegraph*.

9. *How to Have a Sense of Humour about Life:* The Master and Margarita *by Mikhail Bulgakov*

Revered as the best rendition of *The Master and Margarita*, I used Collins Harvill's 1988 edition of Michael Glenny's translation. I've drawn lots of stories and quotes about Bulgakov's life from J. A. E Curtis's compelling collection *Manuscripts Don't Burn: Mikhail Bulgakov – A Life in Letters and Diaries* (Bloomsbury, 1991). This is such an excellent compilation of short diary entries and extracts from the letters. It really makes Bulgakov come alive and is one of my favourite books. See also: *Bulgakov's Last Decade: The Writer as Hero* by J. A. E. Curtis (Cambridge University Press, 2005); and *Between Two Worlds: A Critical Introduction to* The Master and Margarita by Andrew Barratt (Clarendon Press, 1987).

10. *How to Avoid Hypocrisy:* Dead Souls *by Nikolai Gogol*

I worked from the Penguin Classics 2004 edition of *Dead Souls*, translated by Robert A. Maguire. I also used David Magarshack's biography *Gogol: A Life* (Faber and Faber, 1957); *The Enigma of Gogol: An Examination of the Writings of N. V. Gogol and Their Place in the Russian Literary Tradition* by Richard Peace (Cambridge University Press, 2010); *Designing Dead Souls: An Anatomy of Disorder in Gogol* by Susanne Fusso (Stanford University Press, 1993); and *The Creation of Nikolai Gogol* by Donald Fanger (Harvard University Press, 1990). *The Sexual Labyrinth of Nikolai Gogol* by Simon Karlinsky (University of Chicago Press, 1992) is truly superb.

11. *How to Know What Matters in Life:* War and Peace *by Lev Tolstoy*

I used the 2007 Penguin Classics edition of *War and Peace*, translated by Anthony Briggs, with an afterword by Orlando Figes. This is the paperback with *Mademoiselle Caroline Rivière* by Ingres (1805) on the cover.

A Note on Women Writers

I am very torn about the fact that only one woman is featured in this collection. But I wanted this book to be about the lessons taught to us by the Russian classics. And, for good or ill, it is an indisputable fact that most of the books widely acknowledged as 'Russian classics' were written by men.

That said, there were a number of writers I could have considered including. A personal favourite is Irina Ratushinskaya. Her memoir *Grey is the Colour of Hope* is unbelievably entertaining for a book about the author's experiences in a brutal Soviet labour camp in the early 1980s. See also her novels *Fictions and Lies* and *The Odessans*, and her memoir *In the Beginning: The Formative Years of the Dissident Poet*. Sceptre reissued all her work in a beautiful paperback series in 2016.

Lydia Chukovskaya is often cited (as she is here) for her friendship with Anna Akhmatova. Her own writing is great, and I particularly love *The Deserted House* (also known as 'Sofia Petrovna'), a novel about a typist caught up in the horror of the 1930s purges.

I would happily re-read Nadezhda Mandelstam endlessly: her work is funny, wise, tragic and full of emotion. I also recommend investigating (in no particular order) Teffi, Marina

Tsvetaeva, Yevgenia Ginzburg, Lyudmila Ulitskaya, Tatyana Tolstaya and Ludmila Petrushevskaya.

There are many, many more women to discover, not least the non-fiction writers Svetlana Alexievich and Anna Politkovskaya. For contemporary writing by Soviet-born authors living in the US, I am a huge fan of Olga Grushin, Sana Krasikov and Masha Gessen (who all write in English). For more on these and other reading recommendations, see www.vivgroskop.com.

Acknowledgements

I have wanted to write this book for a very long time. In the end, I had to wait for the right people to come along at the right time, which, by coincidence, meant that the book could appear just in time for the hundredth anniversary of the Russian Revolution in late 2017. It could never have happened without the experience and insight of my agent, Cathryn Summerhayes, and my brilliant editor at Fig Tree, Juliet Annan. I feel honoured to have a jacket cover by legendary designer Jon Gray (gray318). The team at Penguin has been hugely supportive, and I'm especially grateful to Annie Hollands, Anna Steadman, Ellie Smith and Sarah Day. Any errors in this book have occurred very much in spite of these good people and are all mine.

Although I have been writing this book in theory in my head for about twenty years, actually writing it in reality meant that I needed to absent myself from normal life for various periods of time. I wouldn't have been able to do that without the generosity of Julia Hobsbawm; Susan and Judith Pollock; and Caroline Ambrose of the Bath Novel Award. Thank you so much for giving me somewhere to escape to when I most needed it. Sorry if I ate and drank everything. (And thank you to Marjorie for the Welsh cakes. I hope I left enough money.)

The inspiration for this project came in part from Pavel Basinsky's work on Tolstoy and Elif Batuman's memoir *The Possessed*. Thank you to both. The enthusiasm of the below-the-line audience at the *Guardian*'s blog on BBC1's *War and Peace* (featuring Pierre's bonkers prison beard) also played a huge role. Thanks to Kate Abbott at *Guardian* TV for having the foresight to commission those reviews. I love working with you, Kate. The ideas in the Pushkin chapter grew out of a lecture I gave for the Insights programme for *Eugene Onegin* at the Royal Opera House, and the inspiration behind the Turgenev chapter was a short story I wrote for Literary Death Match for Adrian Todd Zuniga and Suzanne Azzopardi. I am very grateful for those opportunities.

Thank you to everyone at the library of the School of Slavonic and Eastern European Studies at University College London, where I took my Master's in Russian Studies. I researched many of the chapters in this library. Their selection of Russian books is second to none. I am very proud of my orange cardboard library card, which took several long months to procure but eventually materialized.

A big fat *spasibo* to everyone at London's Pushkin House and the Pushkin House Russian Book Prize, especially Andrew Jack, Clem Cecil and all my fellow trustees, who are always there to remind the world (and me) of Russia's cultural side, especially at the moments when it seems as if politics will engulf us all.

Spasibochki (yes, this is a word – 'sweet, little thank you') to everyone I knew in Russia in the early 1990s, especially Jo and Ruth, friends for life even when pot kettle black is calling. I have thought of you so much while writing this. I have changed the names of some Russian friends I knew from that time to respect people's privacy, but everything recounted in this book is true. Especially big love to Zhenya, Lyubik, Inga and Tanya, who taught me so much during those years.

To all my former colleagues at Russian *Vogue*, especially Aliona Doletskaya and Vika Davydova: thank you. We worked together during a special time. Hat tip to Katya Pavlova, who gave me Pavel Basinsky's book at a time when I really needed it. A deep bow to Mako Abashidze of the British Georgian Chamber of Commerce and Aliona Muchinskaya of Zima, who have had to know me for too long. Belated thanks to Dr Michael Tilby, Irina Kirillova, Natasha Franklin, Dr Jana Howlett and Dr Natasha Kurashova, who had an extremely beneficial impact on my learning of Russian at different, crucial times.

For support, friendship and inspiration while I've been writing this book: Maura Brickell, Elizabeth Day, Annie Deadman, Hannah Droy, Nicky Higby, Julia Hornsby, Sadie Jones, Jane Lindsey, Aleksandra Majerz, Sue Matthias, Alexandra Pringle, Lionel Shriver, Stefan Stern, Dixie Stewart, Kate Taylor. Thank you to Sam Baker and everyone at The Pool. Thanks always to my wonderful friends Jen, Dawn, Lucie, Susan and Claire. Sorry about the Russian food and all the vodka.

The biggest thanks are reserved for my family, especially my mum and dad and my sister Trudy, and all Groskops and Groscops everywhere, not least my 'cousins' who have come back into my life, Karen and Liz. I owe a debt I can never repay to Simon, Will, Vera and Jack. They are the real dearest teeny tiny little VIPs.